Birds&Blooms
Ultimate Guide to Hummingbirds

Male Costa's,
page 174

Table of Contents

ON THE FRONT COVER
Magnificent hummingbird
Photo by Glenn Bartley

ON THE TITLE PAGE
Male ruby-throated hummingbird
Photo by Purnell Hopson

Editorial

ASSOCIATE CREATIVE DIRECTOR
Christina Spalatin

EXECUTIVE EDITOR
Kirsten Schrader

ART DIRECTOR
Kristen Stecklein

ASSOCIATE EDITOR
Julie Kuczynski

CONTRIBUTING EDITOR
Kelly Aiglon

CONTRIBUTING LAYOUT DESIGNER
Jennifer Ruetz

COPY EDITOR
Amy Rabideau Silvers

PRODUCTION COORDINATOR
Jon Syverson

SENIOR RIGHTS ASSOCIATE
Jill Godsey

Contributors

Alison Auth, Lisa Ballard, Kris Drake, Molly Jasinski, Kenn and Kimberly Kaufman, Heather Lamb, Rachael Liska, Rachel Maidl, Melinda Myers, Rob Ripma, Sally Roth, Jill Staake, Kaitlin Stainbrook, Stacy Tornio

© 2020 RDA Enthusiast Brands, LLC.
1610 N. 2nd St., Suite 102, Milwaukee, WI 53212-3906

International Standard Book Number:
978-1-62145-521-9
(Hardcover)
978-1-62145-522-6
(Paperback)

Library of Congress Control Number:
2020936342

Component Number:
118500100H

Printed in China
1 3 5 7 9 10 8 6 4 2
(Hardcover)
3 5 7 9 10 8 6 4
(Paperback)

Male ruby-throat,
page 180

Rufous,
page 208

Welcome!

A source of endless entertainment and wonder, hummingbirds zip in and out of gardens throughout North America, sparking joy with every whir of their wings. Experience the magic of these energetic fliers through the pages of this book. We'll tell you how to create the ultimate hummingbird habitat—and what nectar-packed plants they love most. Learn to make the one sugar-water recipe they can't resist. Take our advice and your yard will be buzzing with hummingbirds in no time.

—THE EDITORS OF
***BIRDS & BLOOMS* MAGAZINE**

CHAPTER 1

Hummingbird Basics & Beyond

The more you know about these incredible creatures, the more you'll savor the moment the next one flutters by. Learn the species, their sounds and how to create a stunning habitat.

Miniature Marvels

Celebrate the high-energy hustle of hummingbirds.

A young ruby-throated hummingbird alights atop a flower stalk.

ROSLYNN LONG

HUMMINGBIRDS SEEM TO EXIST in a different dimension from other birds. If we look around, we can see basic similarities in the lives of sparrows, crows, quail, woodpeckers and just about every other kind of bird. But hummingbirds are different.

They appear to be living in a separate magical world. And the fact that we can often witness the magic show in our own gardens—or even right outside our windows—makes hummingbirds all the more endearing.

Endless Energy

While miniature in dimension, hummingbirds are amazing powerhouses. A ruby-throated or rufous weighs about one-ninth of an ounce. That's lighter than a nickel!

The sight of a hummer darting about the garden is especially impressive when we break this high-speed action down by the numbers. A hummingbird at rest may breathe four times per second, and its heart may beat more than 20 times per second.

A hummingbird may also beat its wings 50 times a second. To get a sense of what this means, stand and flap your arms as fast as you can for a few moments. If you concentrate, you should be able to flap four times in a second. Now imagine doing this same action a whopping 20 times faster—an impossible feat for a human, but nothing remarkable for a tiny hummingbird.

At first glance, hummingbirds often seem delightfully tame, even confiding. Sometimes they'll come astonishingly close, especially if you're near a sugar-water feeder or other nectar source.

Think about it from their perspective, though. Humans must seem like incredibly big, slow creatures to them. They're likely to be more interested in things closer to their own size and speed.

Spiders, for instance, may make you squeamish, but anyone who loves hummingbirds should appreciate spiders. Hummers often use bits of spiderweb to build their nests. Strong, lightweight and super sticky, it's the perfect nest material, allowing for compact nests that will stretch as the baby hummers begin to grow.

Protecting Their Turf

An endless sugar rush fuels all the high-speed comings and goings of these miniature marvels. Many birds feed on nectar, but none do it as consistently as hummingbirds. This dependence on flower nectar drives much of their interesting and acrobatic behavior.

Consider the critical matter of defending territory. A pair of robins will guard a space of an acre or so during the nesting season. This territory will supply food, water

IN THEIR ZONE

Male hummingbirds are often territorial around feeding zones. Above is a male ruby-throated and at right is a female ruby-throated. Both will go to great lengths to defend their turf from other hummingbirds.

and shelter for the pair and their offspring. After the nesting season, though, robins gather in flocks and stop defending their space.

Hummingbirds, in contrast, may defend a temporary feeding territory at any time of year. Flowers produce only so much nectar in a day, so if a hummer finds a good patch of blooms, it may start defending that patch, driving away all other hummers.

All the zooming and chattering of hummingbirds chasing away

rivals may seem like a waste of energy to us, but it may be easier than flying off and finding another flower patch. It becomes somewhat comical, though, when the instinct carries over to hummingbirds visiting feeders. The feeders may have a vast supply of sugar water, but the birds don't see it that way. The instinct to guard their food source is so strong that the hummer wars may continue all day.

The reliance on flowers also drives their migration patterns.

FIGHTING INSTINCTS

Hummingbird battles over territory consist mostly of posturing and bill-pointing, as these two ruby-throated are doing.

In the West, for example, species like the rufous, broad-tailed and Calliope hummingbirds migrate north through the deserts and valleys in very early spring and south through the mountain meadows in late summer. Why? Because that's where the flowers are. In early spring the mountain meadows are still covered with snow, while in late summer the valleys may be hot and dry, so the hummers have adapted their routes to follow the blooming seasons.

Backyard Bustle

One summer, when we discovered a female ruby-throated building a nest in our Ohio backyard, we witnessed an example of just how extraordinary a hummingbird's energy can be.

An hour after finding the first nest, we discovered another nest in the front yard, with two large young almost ready to fly. Since Kimberly had searched for years without ever finding one of these well-camouflaged nests, we were stunned at the coincidence of finding two on the same day.

But the real surprise came a few hours later, when we realized that the same female hummer was tending both nests!

Our little overachiever was building a second nest even while she was feeding two demanding, nearly full-grown nestlings in the first one. And since the male does nothing to help with the nest or the young (as Kimberly often points out to Kenn), this female ruby-throated was doing it all on her own. Her sheer hustle was nothing short of astounding.

That two bird "experts" can still learn something new about a species as common as a ruby-throated is a powerful reminder that no matter how much we think we know, there are still endless discoveries to be made. And we need look no farther than our own backyards to be amazed, impressed, astonished and blessed by even the tiniest of birds.

—*Kenn and Kimberly Kaufman*

IN CONSTANT MOTION

A ruby-throated hummingbird like the one at left is always on the move, especially when nectar-filled blooms like this trumpet vine are nearby. High-speed photography might make the birds seem motionless in midair, but their wings are actually beating dozens of times every second. Above, a rufous hummingbird is perched, and at right two nestling black-chinned hummingbirds get ready to fledge.

The Awe of Hummingbirds

13 jaw-dropping facts and amazing reader photos.

Female ruby-throated hummingbird
Kristi Wenger Stoltzfus
STEELES TAVERN, VIRGINIA

Ruby-throated hummingbird
Carl Leichtenberger
PITTSFIELD, PENNSYLVANIA

❮ 1 They're never on break.
While resting, the average 4-inch hummingbird takes about 150 breaths per minute.

︿ 2 They're powerful fccdcrs.
A hummingbird uses its tongue, which functions as a tiny pump, to suck the sought-after sweet liquid from feeders and flowers.

❯ 3 They go the distance.
Rufous hummingbirds migrate farther than any other North American species. They travel 4,000 miles from Mexico to Alaska every spring.

Rufous hummingbird
Robert Howson
KIRKLAND, WASHINGTON

Anna's hummingbird
Desiree D. Skatvold
LIVERMORE, CALIFORNIA

❮ 4 Their homes are tiny.

The average nest is about the size of a
half-dollar coin. The eggs inside the tiny
structure look like mini white jelly beans.

Rufous hummingbirds
Rod Marr
ABBOTSFORD, BRITISH COLUMBIA

⌃ 5 They're quite protective.

Hummingbirds can be very territorial and will try to protect their food sources—both flowers and feeders. They spend a lot of time chasing other birds away.

❯ 6 They return to you.

Recognize the same hummers at your feeder every year? Banding research shows they're likely to return to the area where they hatched.

Ruby-throated hummingbird
Gary Robinette
SPRINGFIELD, VIRGINIA

Judy Evans

HIGHLANDS RANCH,
COLORADO

❮ 7 They've got wing skills.

Hummingbirds hover in midair at flowers and feeders, and they're the only birds that can fly backward. Their wings move in a figure-eight pattern, allowing for easy maneuvering.

❯ 8 They're talkative.

Some species, specifically male Anna's and Costa's, are regular singers. With other species, the most common sounds are aggressive calls that resemble chattering or squealing. You'll hear them when several hummingbirds are gathered near a food source.

❯ 9 They're amazingly agile.

Rufous hummingbirds are known for erratic movements, beating their wings more than 50 times per second, and even faster in extreme flight mode.

Ruby-throated hummingbird
Deb Forster
CLAYTON, NORTH CAROLINA

Rufous hummingbird
Jeanette Brooks-Milano
CENTRALIA, WASHINGTON

Ruby-throated
hummingbird
Lonna Ours
PETERSBURG,
WEST VIRGINIA

⌃ 10 They fly solo.

Hummingbirds are solitary migrants, so you won't see them traveling in flocks. Wintering grounds vary by species, but most ruby-throated spend the cold months between southern Mexico and northern Panama.

❯ 11 Their diet may vary.

You typically see hummingbirds at nectar blooms and sugar-water feeders, but they also eat tree sap and small insects when flowers are hard to find in the wild.

Ruby-throated hummingbird
Tammi Elbert
WASHINGTON, MISSOURI

Costa's hummingbird
Lisa J. Swanson MARICOPA, ARIZONA

⌃ 12 They love a quick refresh.

A birdbath with a small mister, bubbler or sprayer attracts hummingbirds. It's a rare sight, but they might fly through the mist of a lawn sprinkler, too!

Broad-tailed hummingbird
Jennifer Plunkett ARVADA, COLORADO

⌃ 13 They're nesting pros.

It takes less than a week (about five to seven days) for a hummingbird to build its nest. Built by females only, nests are made of lichen, moss and spiderwebs.

Amazing Traits

Yes, hummingbirds have the ability to fly backward. And so much more.

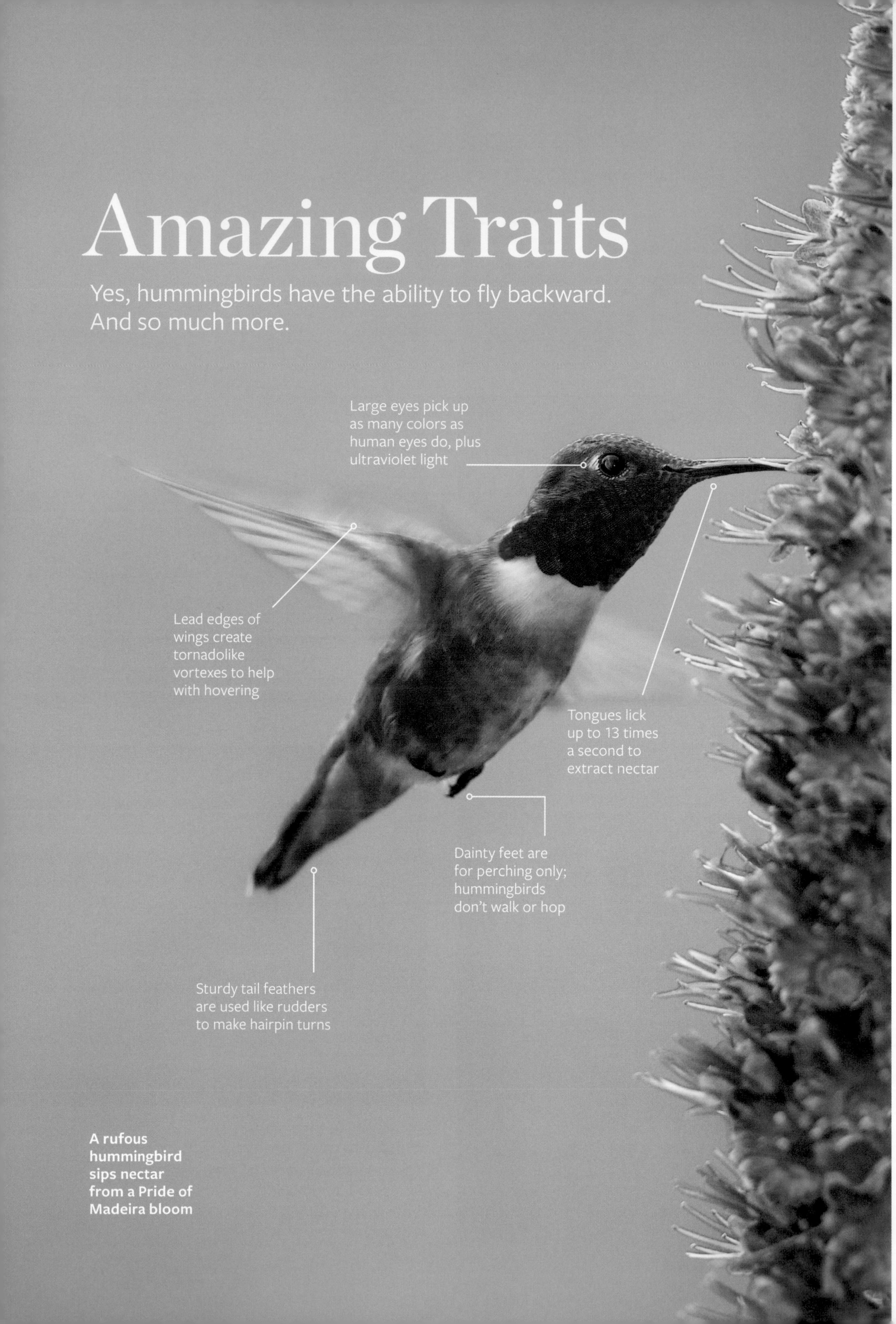

Large eyes pick up as many colors as human eyes do, plus ultraviolet light
Lead edges of wings create tornadolike vortexes to help with hovering
Tongues lick up to 13 times a second to extract nectar
Dainty feet are for perching only; hummingbirds don't walk or hop
Sturdy tail feathers are used like rudders to make hairpin turns

A rufous hummingbird sips nectar from a Pride of Madeira bloom

JIMMY PHU HUYNH/SHUTTERSTOCK

A Hummingbird Home

Zoom in on one of these teeny-tiny nests and tour its artful structure.

The female smooths and shapes the inside of the nest using her body.

Lichens, mosses, plant down and fibers make up the nest and camouflage its exterior.

Her nest is big enough for two eggs, and incubation lasts 12 to 19 days.

She collects and weaves stretchy spider silk through the nest to hold it together, bind it to the branch and give it the ability to expand as the chicks grow.

Most nests are built in the fork of a tree or shrub, 10 to 40 feet above the ground.

WORLD'S BEST MOM

When it comes to the job of parenting, female hummingbirds do all the heavy lifting, from building the nest to raising the young. After both eggs hatch, the mother feeds her nestlings a slurry of nectar and keeps them warm. Once they're about 15 days old, she starts bringing them small insects, continuing to care for them until about a week after they leave the nest.

The Life of a Female Hummingbird

Talk about girl power. Female hummingbirds are bona fide multitaskers, flitting from one vital activity to another in an effort to keep the whole family fed, safe and secure.

Ruby-throated hummingbird

PENNSYLVANIA

COSTA RICA

W

HEN IT COMES TO hummingbirds, the spotlight is usually on the flashy, colorful males. The females, more subtly colored and less flamboyant in their actions, are often underappreciated. But it's the females that actually lead more active and interesting lives than their mates. We decided to demonstrate by following one typical ruby-throated hummingbird on her journey from wintering grounds through the first part of the nesting season.

Winter in the Tropics

The story begins in late January in Central America, along the foothills of Costa Rica, where a female ruby-throat arrived in October from her summer nesting territory in Pennsylvania. Here in the tropics, the weather is warm, flowers bloom everywhere, and it's always easy to find tiny insects to eat. Nearly a dozen other species of hummingbirds are living nearby, in the forest or along the edge where this ruby-throat spends her time, but mostly they live without direct competition.

This bird has had an easy time of it for the last three months, but soon she'll start to become restless, and her instincts will tell her to go north.

Heading Home

First the heroine of our story begins gaining weight. This is a good thing, because the fat she puts on will fuel her migratory flight. During some seasons, ruby-throated hummers can double their body mass in about a week, going from about a 10th of an ounce up to a fifth.

In late February she begins moving north through Central America. Traveling by day and sleeping at night, she flies out of

Ruby-throated hummingbird

Costa Rica and through Nicaragua, Honduras and Guatemala. Then she heads for southeast Mexico. It's a leisurely trip, covering about 1,500 miles in six weeks.

When she reaches the north coast of Mexico's Yucatan Peninsula in mid-April, she faces a major challenge. The shortest route north now is directly across the Gulf of Mexico—600 miles over open water. Even with favorable winds, the flight will take her about 18 hours. Many other migrants are traveling the same route at this season, including small songbirds, but it's an extraordinary journey for a creature weighing less than a nickel. When she completes the crossing, arriving on the U.S. Gulf Coast, she must quickly find food so she can build up her strength and keep flying north.

Nesting Grounds

The female ruby-throated hummer reaches central Pennsylvania the second week of May. Her summer territory is in a suburban neighborhood with flower gardens and plenty of trees. Males have already arrived. A few are in the neighborhood, each one fiercely defending a small territory by perching high, chasing away intruders and performing courtship displays.

Unlike many songbirds, the female ruby-throated won't select a mate and move in to share his territory. She establishes her own little home range and mates with one of the nearby males. And after the first date, her Prince Charming won't pay any more attention to her. He'll be off trying to court other females, leaving each new mate to start raising her young by herself.

Starting a Family

In the third week of May, the ruby-throated chooses a site for her nest.

HATCHING HER PLAN

Female hummingbirds do all the work of nest building and raising their young by themselves. Here you can see the progression of tiny eggs becoming two baby hummers about to fledge the nest.

LEFT: LEAMAN PHOTOGRAPHY; RIGHT: (4) RICHARD DAY/DAYBREAK IMAGERY

Typically it's out near the tip of a long horizontal tree branch 15 to 20 feet above the ground. The construction of a hummingbird nest is amazing. First she carefully gathers scraps of spiderweb to form a sticky pad on a branch. To this she'll affix a flat pad of plant down before building up the sides of the nest with more of the same soft, pliable materials. It may take her hundreds of trips over a week or more to gather what she needs and press it into place. As a finishing touch, she'll select tiny flakes of lichen to camouflage the outside of the miraculous little cup.

After the nest is done, she lays a tiny egg and soon begins incubating it. One to three days later, she lays a second one. For the next two weeks or so, she will sit on them all night and most of the day, leaving the nest several times a day to feed herself.

When the eggs hatch, our already industrious little bird turns into a dynamo.

The ruby-throated visits flowers, drinking as much nectar as she can gather and swallowing tiny insects as well. Then she returns to the nest and sticks her bill deep into the throat of a baby, pumping her neck muscles as she regurgitates the nectar mix into its stomach. Then she feeds the other baby. If it's chilly, she may sit on top of the young for a minute to brood them and warm them up. Then she's off again. It requires an exhausting effort to get enough food for herself and both of her young.

An Empty Nest

For about three weeks the baby hummers grow, and the tiny nest, with its spiderweb magic, actually stretches to accommodate them.

They begin exercising their wings after about 15 days, standing up on the edge of the nest and buzzing their wings vigorously. A few days later, one at a time, they abruptly leave the nest, launching into an awkward first flight.

At first the fledglings can't feed themselves; it takes practice to hover at a flower and drink nectar. The female continues to feed them for up to a week after they leave the nest as they learn how to find food. At the same time, our tireless little mother may already be building another nest in order to raise a second brood for the season.

What they lack in flash and finery, these feathered sprites make up for in spunk, determination and fine parenting skills. So the next time you see a female hummingbird, be sure to give her a little extra attention. She's earned it!

HOW YOU CAN HELP
Want to lend female hummingbirds a hand? Try these tips:

1. Keep your sugar-water feeder full. If it's empty, the birds will look for food somewhere else.

2. Offer more than one feeder. Yes, hummingbirds can get protective over feeders in summer. Help defeat a bully male hummingbird by hanging feeders in a couple of locations.

3. Keep your feeders clean. You should change the water every few days and clean your feeder once a week to keep it as free of bugs and grime as possible.

4. Plant nectar-rich flowers. Females can use every nectar source they can get.

Before migrating, the young may fuel up on butterfly weed.

Ruby-throated
hummingbird

Sensational Sounds

From wing beats to sweet songs, this is what you should listen for.

Q**UESTION: WHY DOES A HUMMINGBIRD HUM?** Answer: Because it can't remember the words!

Okay, that's a pretty bad joke, but it addresses an interesting point. The humming for which hummingbirds are named isn't a vocal sound, but one created by the rapid beating of their wings. This isn't the only sound hummingbirds make. Here's what to listen for.

The male Anna's hummingbird is a champion singer.

Regular Calls

All hummingbirds make short, soft callnotes. These are often useful for identifying species. In the West, for example, the soft *teew* of the black-chinned hummingbird is very different from the musical chip of a rufous hummingbird or the thin tic of a Costa's hummingbird.

Aggressive Calls

Hummingbirds are amazingly feisty creatures, constantly sparring over choice flower patches and feeders. Their aerial battles are mostly just bluffing, but they pump up the effect with all kinds of chattering, squealing noises. When a large number of hummingbirds gather, most of the sounds that you hear will be these aggressive calls.

Intriguing Songs

Yes, some hummingbirds do sing! The champion singer among North American hummers is the male Anna's hummingbird, which is very common along the Pacific Coast. He will sit on a high perch and sing for minutes at a time—typically a scratchy series of notes punctuated by a loud *tzzip, tzzip!* He can do this without opening his mouth very wide. In the desert Southwest, the male Costa's hummingbird also sings, but with a thin, piercing whistle instead.

Although many kinds of tropical hummingbirds have noteworthy songs, most of those in North America aren't as accomplished as the Anna's or Costa's hummers. For example, what passes for song from the male ruby-throated hummingbird is just a monotonous series of calls, given mostly at dawn.

Wing and Tail Sounds

Many hummingbird sounds are produced by the feathers of the wings or tail vibrating against the air. The male broad-tailed hummingbird of the Rocky Mountain region has an especially impressive sound. You can always tell when he flies past because of the high, metallic trilling of his wings.

While the male ruby-throated's wing sounds are not as obvious, the pointed outer feathers of his wings create a high-pitched whine during his flight displays, and the shorter inner feathers make a rattling sound when he changes directions.

The male Anna's hummingbird is famous for his song, but he also produces a remarkable sound with his tail feathers.

His courtship display includes a dramatic zooming dive, in which he plummets toward the ground and then pulls up with a loud, explosive pop that can be heard from hundreds of yards away. Scientists used to debate whether this was a vocal sound, but studies have shown that it's the outer tail feathers vibrating at the bottom of the dive making the noise.

Listen carefully the next time you see a hummingbird flitting around the garden. Not only will you hear that familiar hum of those super fast-beating wings, but you just may hear a joyful serenade.

SHINY & BRIGHT

When the sun hits it just right, a male ruby-throated hummingbird's gorget, or throat, is a beautiful irridescent red. His vibrant green head glows, too.

Flashes of Red

Quick! Prep your feeders and fill your garden with tubular flowers for a chance to see ruby-throated hummingbirds, one of the most popular fliers in the East.

SEVERAL HUMMINGBIRD SPECIES ARE scattered across the western half of North America, but only one, the ruby-throated, flies the eastern skies regularly. As the region's tiniest bird, this species generates a lot of excitement when it alights in your backyard.

Males steal the show with their green bodies and ruby red throats that glisten like jewels in the sunlight. Females aren't as grandiose in appearance. They sport green backs, white underparts and black masks near their eyes. All juveniles look so similar to females that it's nearly impossible to tell which it is.

Ruby-throateds zip, zoom and dart through gardens, woodland edges and parks from one food source to another. Because they constantly burn energy while on the move, they may eat up to three times their body weight in a day. To find that much nectar, one bird might visit hundreds of flowers per day, which is why a hummingbird-friendly backyard is so important.

Attracting ruby-throateds is easy when you cater to their sweet tooth with feeders and flowers. A sugar-water feeder is the quickest way to jump-start your hummingbird haven. Your best bet: a basic red plastic feeder with a built-in ant moat and yellow bee guards; they keep pests away and your fast-flying guests safe.

Fill your feeders with a mixture of 4 parts water to 1 part table sugar. Boil the mix and let it cool. Although hummingbirds love red, it's not necessary (and may even be harmful) to dye your mix red with food coloring. Clear sugar water gets the job done just as well.

Nectar-rich tubular flowers are another way for backyard birders in the east to easily lure ruby-throateds. Bee balm, salvia, coral honeysuckle and fuchsia are popular with hummingbirds, offering the vibrant colors they love and easy access to nectar.

However, the sweet sustenance takes care of just one dietary need. Ruby-throated hummingbirds also require protein to survive, and they get their fill of it from small insects, such as mosquitoes, gnats and fruit flies. They eat spiders, too.

Food sources like sugar water, flowers and bugs are especially important for young ruby-throats as they seek nutrition and prepare for fall migration. Males tend to start the trek first, sometimes heading south as early as July. Watch for flashes of ruby as these eastern favorites take off.

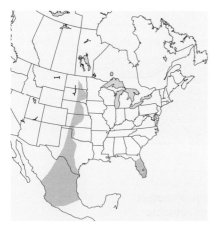

RANGE MAP KEY

▨ Winter	▨ Summer	▨ Year-Round	▨ Migration

RUBY-THROATED HUMMINGBIRD

Archilochus colubris

LENGTH: 3¾ inches.

WINGSPAN: 4½ inches.

DISTINCTIVE MARKINGS: Ruby red throat on male; both sexes have a showy metallic green back and head.

VOICE: Faint; a very rapid series of chipping notes.

HABITAT: Areas with plenty of colorful, nectar-rich flowers.

NESTING: Builds a cup-shaped nest the diameter of a quarter and camouflages it with lichens. Lays two tiny white eggs.

DIET: Nectar, insects and tree sap.

BACKYARD FAVORITES: Sugar water and bright, trumpet-shaped flowers.

BIRD BRAINS

Colorful rufous hummingbirds, like this male, have amazing memories. They often seek out and stop at the same feeders and flowers during their annual migration routes.

Toughest Bird on the Block

Get to know the feisty and smart rufous hummingbird.

F YOU RESIDE IN A northwestern state, like Washington or Oregon, and see a rumble break out at your sugar-water feeder, a male rufous hummingbird is the likely culprit. Known for their aggressive nature, rufous males are particularly antagonistic during the late-spring breeding season when territories are being established. Female rufous hummingbirds also jump into the fray to protect nesting territories and to drive off other rufous that get too close. They've even been known to chase chipmunks away.

Rufous are hard to miss as they zip, zoom and dive around sugar-water feeders. Male rufous hummingbirds have orange

backs and bellies and iridescent red throats, while females and juveniles sport more subdued green coloring. The Allen's hummingbird, another species of the West, is often confused for the rufous. As a general rule of thumb, if the male's back is more orange than green, it's a rufous. Females and juveniles of both species are essentially identical.

During courtship, a male rufous dives in a J-shaped or steep oval pattern when a female enters his breeding territory. The male rufous doesn't stick with one female, instead pairing up with multiple partners in a single season.

That means the tough job of parenting falls entirely to the female rufous. She chooses a suitable nesting site and builds the small cup-shaped nest herself using plant matter, such as lichen, moss and bark. She then lays two white jelly bean-sized eggs.

The mother feeds her two young until they're ready to leave the nest, about 21 days after hatching.

In western and southwestern states, it's easy to attract these feisty little birds with sugar-water feeders. Skip the red dye, though, and make your own by combining 1 part table sugar to 4 parts water.

To keep the peace at backyard feeders, set up more than one and place each feeder at a distance and out of sight of the other. If multiple

feeders are available, an aggressive rufous is more willing to share.

Another option is to plant a few nectar-rich red blooms, such as bee balm and penstemon. Tube-shaped blooms also work well.

Even if you're outside their range, a rufous may still visit your yard. Of all western hummingbird species, the rufous is most likely to wander off the typical course. In their southward migration in late summer and fall, rufous spread out across the western half of the continent, and some stray farther. They've been spotted in fall in every eastern state, and dozens spend the winter flitting along the Gulf Coast.

RUFOUS SIGHTINGS

Although uncommon, a rufous hummingbird occasionally finds its way into the southeastern United States.

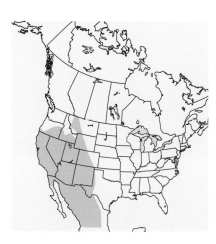

RANGE MAP KEY

Winter   Summer   Year-Round   Migration

RUFOUS HUMMINGBIRD

Selasphorus rufus

LENGTH: 3¾ inches.

WINGSPAN: 4½ inches.

DISTINCTIVE MARKINGS: Male is reddish brown on back, head and tail; scarlet throat. Female is metallic green above, with pale rust-colored sides.

VOICE: Call note is *chewp chewp.*

HABITAT: Open areas and along woodland edges.

NESTING: May nest in loose colonies, with up to 10 nests.

DIET: Nectar and tree sap.

BACKYARD FAVORITES: Attracted to red flowers; sugar water at feeders.

WINGING IT

Anna's, like other hummingbirds, are unable to walk or hop with their small legs.
To move even a fraction of an inch on a perch, they take off and land in their desired spot.

West Coast Cuties

Full feeders and fanciful flowers keep Anna's hummingbirds in backyards year-round.

A STOCKY, MEDIUM-SIZED HUMMINGBIRD, the Anna's is quite a looker. It has a straight, short bill and broad tail that extends past the wings. With bold, metallic greens above a gray belly, Anna's is the only North American hummingbird sporting a full reddish crown.

Males proudly display a brilliant magenta throat, called a gorget, and crown. Females have specks of pink-red on their throats, often forming a small gorget. Their backs are duller, iridescent green, with gray underparts.

To attract a mate a male puts on an aerial display that starts with hovering a few yards in front of a female. He ascends above the treetops, then dives toward the ground, pulling up with a loud screech made by his tail feathers. He does the same to intimidate intruders (including people).

Males also sing to attract mates, something rare among northern temperate hummingbirds, though their squeaks and buzzes are hardly musical to the human ear.

Anna's hummingbirds breed in winter and spring. After mating, the female uses spider silk to bind pieces of plants, hair, feathers and lichen to make a nest. Her two pearly eggs hatch in two weeks, and chicks fledge three weeks later.

Anna's range and numbers have grown thanks to feeders and their attraction to both ornamental and native flowers. During the early 1900s, they were found primarily in northern Baja California and southern California. Anna's now reside as far north as British Columbia and even wander north to Alaska. Their range also extends eastward into Arizona, Nevada, Utah and western Texas, though they've been spotted as far away as New York and Newfoundland.

The growing and blooming cycles of native, coastal chaparral plants match the breeding and feeding habits of Anna's—critical pollinators in these ecosystems. This beneficial relationship is one reason Anna's are adapted to nesting in winter and early spring along the coast. In other seasons they may seek higher elevations in search of food, or migrate east and west across California and Arizona.

Like many other hummingbirds, Anna's eat insects such as midges and leaf hoppers. Their high-protein diet might help them tolerate colder conditions in gardens, parks and streamside areas all along the West Coast throughout the entire year.

RANGE MAP KEY

■ Winter	■ Summer	■ Year-Round	■ Migration

ANNA'S HUMMINGBIRD
Calypte anna

LENGTH: 4 inches.

WINGSPAN: 5¼ inches.

DISTINCTIVE MARKINGS: Adult males have an iridescent red crown and throat. Females have a red patch on the throat and white markings over eyes.

VOICE: Call is a high sharp *stit*.

HABITAT: Lush gardens and parks that provide nectar-producing flowers.

NESTING: Made of plant down held together with spider webs. Females lay two small white eggs.

DIET: Nectar, sugar water, spiders, small insects and tree sap.

BACKYARD FAVORITE: Sugar water.

The Fabulous 10!

More than 350 hummingbird species buzz around the American tropics, yet the majority are quite rare. Here are 10 colorful characters you could spot nesting in the U.S.

‹ The Dark Knight
MAGNIFICENT

Another large species, the male magnificent looks dark and mysterious until the light catches his brilliant purple cap and green throat. Females are duller gray and green. This species spends the summer in southwest mountain forests.

⌄ The Wing-Singer
BROAD-TAILED

In western mountain meadows, you know the male broad-tailed is coming because his wings make a musical, metallic trilling sound when he flies. He's emerald green on the back and sides, and rosy red on the throat. Females are plainer, mostly green and white with orange sides.

‹ The Tropical Texan
BUFF-BELLIED

Down in southern Texas, this medium-large hummingbird is seen all year, and it sometimes wanders along the Gulf Coast. Males and females look almost the same: pale buff on the belly, rusty red on the tail, and apple green on the back, throat and chest.

WALLFLOWERS IN FOCUS
Female hummingbirds aren't as flashy, but they deserve a look!

Adult male hummingbirds are colorful showoffs and typically easy to identify. But the females and juveniles of most North American species look the same: greenish on the back and whitish or grayish on the underparts, with small white spots on the tail feathers. It takes an expert to identify subtle differences in shape, color and callnotes. So don't fret if a female or juvenile has you stumped.

⌃ The Tiny Marvel

CALLIOPE

North America's smallest bird, the Calliope is barely longer than 2 inches. The male is known by his striped throat, with rays of red-violet and white. Females are tiny and plain. Spending the summer in the northwest, Calliopes go to Mexico for the winter.

❮ The Look-Alike

ALLEN'S

Nearly identical to the rufous, Allen's live mainly along the California coast, although they spread eastward during migration. Adult males have a bright green center back, instead of coppery brown. Females and young ones are almost impossible to identify.

‹ The Arizona Gem
BROAD-BILLED

Shining dark green and blue, with a bright red bill, the male broad-bill is hard to miss in a few parts of southern Arizona but is hardly ever seen elsewhere. The female has a plain gray belly.

⌄ The Flashy Giant
BLUE-THROATED

Almost the size of a sparrow, the blue-throated is the largest breeding hummingbird in the U.S. It lives along shady canyons in mountains near the Mexican border. The blue on its throat is hard to see, but its spectacular tail pattern is obvious: blue-black with big white patches.

❮ The Desert Dweller

COSTA'S

In Southern California and Arizona, this tough little bird manages to find flowers even in the desert. The male wears a purple cap and a purple throat patch that flares out to the sides. In early spring, he sings a thin, whistled song, sometimes while zooming through the air in a courtship-display dive.

⌄ The Splash of White

VIOLET-CROWNED

Many hummingbirds have whitish bellies, but the bright violet-crowned is the only one that's snowy white from chin to undertail. The red bill and purple cap are bonus marks. Violet-crowneds are seen mainly in summer along rivers in southern Arizona and southwestern New Mexico.

⌃ The Border Bandit

LUCIFER

A curved bill and flaring purple throat patch mark the male Lucifer. Females have buff or pale rust-colored throats. These birds are distinctive summer residents of dry canyons near the border from western Texas to southern Arizona.

The Mystery of Sphinx Moths

They look like hummingbirds—and act like them, too. Here's how to spot the difference.

A white-lined sphinx moth sticks out its proboscis, ready to feed on foxglove.

WATCH SPHINX MOTHS flitting around your flowers and you'll know why they're often called hummingbird moths. Some species look so much like the tiny birds, right down to the green body and whirring wings, that it's easy to mistake one for a hovering hummer. You also may know sphinx moths as hawk moths, because their streamlined wings make them fast and agile fliers.

Some sphinx species take the day shift, while others work after the sun goes down. Clear-winged types mimic hummingbirds, bees or wasps, flying only during the day. They hover to feed at plants such as butterfly bush (*Buddleia davidii*), honeysuckle vines (*Lonicera sempervirens*) or other flowers that are nectar-rich.

Dusk through dark is prime time for most sphinx species. That's when to look for five-spotted hawk moths hovering at petunias, hostas, four-o'clocks, and other tubular flowers. Night fliers, including the banded sphinx, start their shift at dark. Moths such as the white-lined sphinx and nessus sphinx are busiest when the sun sinks but pull double duty and also seek nectar during the day.

To maximize the sphinx moth population in your backyard, simply grow a variety of plants that bloom in both day and night hours. Like hummingbirds, sphinx moths prefer tube-shaped flowers with nectar in the base of the petals, such as columbines, nasturtiums and four-o'clocks. That structure prevents many other pollinators from draining the nectar dry, so the chance of a payoff is much greater than in daisies or other flowers that butterflies or bees easily visit.

Also of note: Sphinx moths have a secret weapon. It's an extra-long proboscis, or drinking straw, that is sometimes twice the length of their body. The proboscis allows them to reach nectar that other pollinators can't.

Clearwing sphinx moth

CURIOUS MOVEMENT

Tickle a sphinx moth caterpillar and the larva will rear up defensively, curling its head while the rest of its body remains flat. This is the same posture taken by the mythical beasts that guard pharaohs' tombs.

Unlike hummingbirds, sphinx moths don't zero in on red. Tubular flowers of any color lure day-fliers, while fragrant white or light-colored blossoms hail the sphinx moth squad in the evening by both sight and scent. Flowers such as four-o'clocks and moonflowers that open late in the day or at night, or that release a stronger fragrance at night, such as honeysuckle and petunias, attract the evening shift. Plant a trellis of moonflower vine (*Ipomoea alba*) or place a potted datura on your patio to watch the blossoms unfurl at dusk. If you're lucky, moths arrive minutes later.

Choosing moth-friendly blooms is worth the effort when the reward is a glance at one of these peculiar fliers. The wings of clear-winged sphinx moths, such as the snowberry clearwing, become apparent soon after emerging from the cocoon. Other species conceal their beauty under a pair of brown or gray patterned top wings for protective coloration. When open wide, their underwings are surprisingly beautiful—often a rosy pink, sometimes with deep blue eyespots as sported by the twin-spotted sphinx.

No matter how gorgeous the adults, the larvae evoke a "Yuck!" from many folks, although not from birds, which eagerly devour them. When full-grown, the caterpillars are about the size of your little finger and are smooth with a pointy horn at the tail end.

It's normal to overlook the unseemly larvae entirely unless one happens to cross your path as it wanders off to pupate in the late summer or early fall. Or you may only notice its presence when you see your tomato leaves devoured by a hungry caterpillar.

All that being said, it's a real treat when an adult sphinx chooses to feed on backyard plants. Whether you watch one at your flowers during the day or catch a glimpse of one darting through the night, the secrets of the sphinx moths are a thrill to uncover.

CREATURE OF HABIT

The big poplar sphinx, with wings 4 to nearly 6 inches across, has no proboscis at all. It never feeds in its adult stage, and emerges only to locate a mate and start the next generation.

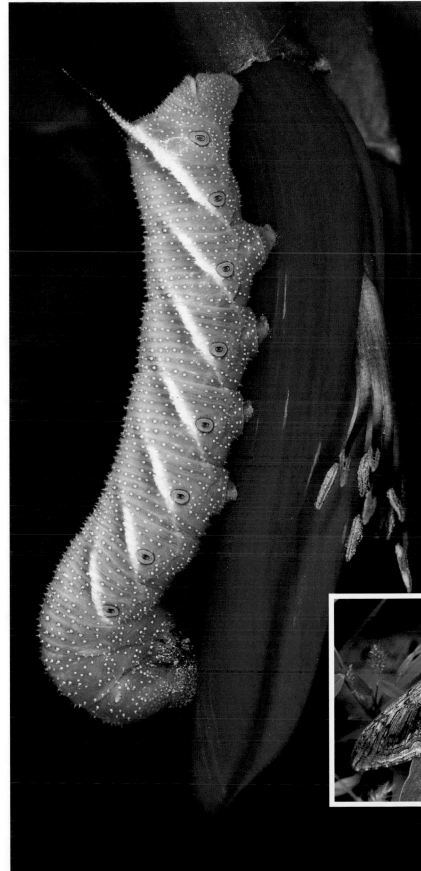

18 PLANTS THAT ATTRACT SPHINX MOTHS

Nectar plants	Host plants
Brugmansia	Grapevine
Butterfly bush	Honeysuckle
Columbine	Poplar (*Populus* species, including cottonwood, poplar, aspen)
Datura	
Evening primrose	
Flowering tobacco (*Nicotiana*)	Snowberry (*Symphoricarpos* species)
Four-o'clocks	Virginia creeper
Honeysuckle	Tomato
Hosta	
Moonflower vine (*Ipomoea alba*)	
Nasturtium	
Verbena	

Five-spotted hawk moth caterpillar, also known as a tomato hornworm (left) and adult moth (above).

CHAPTER 2

Feeding 101

Hummingbirds are always on the lookout for their next meal. Get into their minds and learn about feeders. Soon you'll have hummers literally eating out of your hands.

A ruby-throated
hummingbird sits on
Faye Chapel salvia.

Feeder Tips & Tricks

Here's how to make your backyard a sugar-water hot spot for hungry hummers.

The straight and slender bill of a rufous plunges into a feeder.

Ruby-throated hummers jockey for a spot at a feeder. Bold red blooms, like azaleas are also magnets for hummingbirds.

I**T'S A MAGICAL MOMENT** when a hummingbird comes to call. These flying dynamos, arguably the crown jewels of backyard birds, are among nature's most beautiful and fascinating creatures. Once you know what they're looking for, hosting them in your backyard is easy. Time to put out the welcome mat!

Go Red

With one of the fastest metabolisms in the animal kingdom, hummingbirds are always on the lookout for nectar to fuel their busy bodies. As it turns out, hummingbirds have a heightened visual sensitivity to red flowers, so they tend to visit blooms in these hues. Perennials like cardinal flower, bee balm and garden phlox; and annuals like flowering tobacco, snapdragon and pentas are excellent varieties to plant. Another option is to set out a bright red feeder or tie a large red bow to one.

Make a Sugary Mix

Hummingbirds love sugar water. Bird expert, author and longtime *Birds & Blooms* contributor George Harrison recommends making the perfect batch by mixing 1 part sugar (no artificial sweeteners, please) with 4 parts water. Bring to a boil, cool completely and then fill your feeder. Leftovers may be refrigerated for up to a week, so consider making extra. Trust us: The hummingbirds can't get enough once they get a taste of the sweet stuff.

A bee guard keeps bees out but allows this rufous's beak in.

Calliope hummingbird

Keep Things Tidy

Ensure that contents stay fresh by filling feeders halfway and changing the mixture every three to five days. Keeping a feeder out of the hot sun also helps. If a feeder does develop mold inside, clean it with hot water and vinegar or a mild detergent. For tough spots, use a bottle brush, or fill the feeder with sand and water and shake vigorously.

Banish Bees

Avoid unwanted guests by choosing a feeder specially designed to them. "Feeder ports should be large enough for a hummingbird's beak but small enough that a bee can't crawl through them," says H. Ross Hawkins, founder and executive director of The Hummingbird Society. "Ideally, the nectar should sit far enough below the port opening, ¼ to ½ inch, so that bees can't access it. While many feeders don't address this problem, basin-style ones are usually excellent in this department."

Trick the Bullies

Sure, they look sweet, but these birds can get downright territorial when food is on the line. To prevent one hummingbird from alienating swarms of others, set two or three feeders out of sight from one another. Problem solved.

Put Out Protein

Besides the carbohydrates that nectar provides, hummingbirds crave protein from insects. "Put a few chunks of banana, melon or other overripe fruit into a mesh bag, such as an old onion bag," suggests author and bird expert Laura Erickson. "Fruit flies may gather, and you can watch your hummingbirds dart about to catch them in midair. Plus, cleanup is a snap because you can throw the bag away when done."

Sugar-Water Setup

First concoct the sweetness. Then fill your feeder of choice. Check out these options!

The Recipe

If you haven't memorized a sugar-water recipe yet, then now is the time. Combine 4 parts hot water to 1 part sugar. Mix until it's completely dissolved. Once it cools to room temperature, it's ready.

Boiling Point

Using really hot water will usually suffice. If you plan on making extra sugar water to store in the fridge or you have so-so water quality, then it's best to boil.

Honey Do or Honey Don't?

Some people like to come up with creative ways to sweeten their sugar water without sugar, and the most common stand-in is honey. Not only is honey a bad idea in general, but it can also make your sugar-water mixture ferment more quickly. Skip the honey and stick to sugar.

The Red Dye Debate

Even though every bird authority around the country seems to agree that you don't need red dye in your sugar water, people continue to add it. You may also see companies offering to sell red sugar water. If this is you, don't feel bad—but it's time for a bit of clarity. You don't need red water to attract hummingbirds. In fact, the red dye could be bad for our bird friends (scientists are still figuring this one out). Either way, it's not worth the risk.

Important Extras

Sugar water eventually goes bad, unless you're lucky enough to have a busy feeder that the hummingbirds quickly empty. You should be in the habit of changing it every few days or even sooner if it's really hot out. Also, don't forget to clean your feeders occasionally. Mold can collect, so you want to make sure you're offering hummingbirds clean, safe water.

Horizontal Bar Feeder

Multiple ports on a bar feeder can mean many hummingbirds at once, which is always a treat. But cross your fingers that these territorial birds make friends instead of foes. Prevent any power trips by setting up several feeders.

Classic Plastic Feeder

Hummingbird newbies can't go wrong using a standard sugar-water feeder. While there's nothing fancy about this backyard staple, the plastic is easy to clean and the bright red color is naturally attracts hummingbirds. Many of these classics come with a built-in ant moat, which prevents hungry pests from crawling inside to sample the sweet stuff.

Saucer Feeder

Flying saucer-shaped feeders are backyard favorites for a reason. They're super easy to clean and refill, and the sugar water is usually far enough below the feeding ports that pesky bugs can't dive in for a snack. Built-in ant moats provide additional protection.

BUILT-IN ANT MOAT

Artsy Glass Feeder

If you already have a robust and hungry hummingbird population in your yard, try a feeder with a bit more flair. Chic and stylish glass feeders like this one may be a challenge to clean, and there's no perch for the birds to linger on. However, it's a fun option for watching how hummingbirds hover.

Pests Be Gone!

Discover seven natural ways to keep backyard bugs away from feeders.

Male calliope hummingbird

Calliope hummingbirds flutter happily at a feeder.

F EEDERS FILLED WITH SUGAR water attract sweet tooths, such as hummingbirds and orioles. But other not-so-welcome guests, including ants, wasps and bees, sometimes crawl in and create problems. "You can deter insects while remembering they're part of nature, too," says Emma Greig, the project leader for Project FeederWatch of the Cornell Lab of Ornithology.

Frustrated backyard birders may be tempted to use pesticides or oils to keep bugs away. Emma advises against it because they may harm the birds, as well as the bees whose populations are declining. Instead, try these all-natural solutions.

- Choose red saucer feeders. With their long tongues, hummingbirds can reach the nectar—but insects can't. While hummingbirds prefer the color red, bees are attracted to yellow.
- Attach an ant moat, typically about 3 inches wide and 1 to 2 inches deep. Because ants can't swim, water is an effective deterrent. You can make a moat or buy feeders with one built in. Keep them clean and filled with water.
- Hang feeders with fishing line, which is too thin for ants to climb.
- Slip nectar guard tips over hummingbird feeder holes. The nectar guards block insects like yellow jackets, but hummingbirds can still get to the nectar. You can buy them or create your own mesh guard out of an onion bag.
- Periodically move the feeders by 3 or 4 feet. Birds will still find them, but insects often won't.
- Hang a few fake wasp nests in protected areas to deter real wasps, which are territorial and won't typically venture into a place they think is already occupied.
- Plant bee- and hummingbird-friendly food sources in hanging baskets and in your garden. Try annuals like fuchsia and impatiens; and perennials like trumpet vine, bee balm and milkweed.
- Try a leak-free feeder and prevent the summer heat from causing nectar to expand and leak out.

BYE-BYE, ANTS AND BEES

Readers share tips for keeping feeders free from unwelcome guests.

Insert a Q-tip in one of the drinking ports, letting the tip stick out. The nectar travels up the stem to the cotton, and the wasps and bees will sit on the tip and not bother the other feeding ports.

Dell Kyle
FAYETTEVILLE, GEORGIA

Bee guards work great for me. They are like little cages that fit into the feeder holes. The hummingbird's bill slides in and out easily, but it keeps the bees from reaching the sugar water.

Rebecca Williamson
BUSHNELL, ILLINOIS

To prevent ants from taking over your feeders, rub a very small coat of Vicks VapoRub on whatever your feeder hangs from. I've found that it doesn't bother the birds and the ants won't go near it.

Ruth Andren
GREENE, MAINE

Protect your feeder from ants by stringing it up with 8-lb. fishing line. The line is too narrow for the ants to traverse. I've used this trick successfully for many years.

Elizabeth Hodges
CLEMSON, SOUTH CAROLINA

Poke a hole in the middle of an old spray can cap. Run a wire to hang the feeder through the hole and put a dab of waterproof glue around the wire to prevent the ants from sneaking through. Then fill the cap with water.

Lisa Barlet
NEWBURG, NORTH DAKOTA

FROM LEFT: JOHN GILL; CHRISTINE HAINES

Hand-Feed Hummingbirds

Experience the thrill of tiny bird feet perched on your finger.

IT'S NOT HARD to find plenty of videos online of lucky people hand-feeding hummingbirds. It's incredible to watch. And if you've always yearned for the excitement of seeing delicate hummingbirds up close, here's how you can do it, too.

Be Present

The easiest way to get in on the action is to be in the middle of it. Study the traffic at your hummingbird feeder and find out when it's busiest (usually after dawn and before dusk). If you have multiple feeders, remove all but one. Then, put a bench or lawn chair beside the feeder and sit as still as possible. Try this often and eventually your presence will be accepted and, ultimately, ignored.

Lend a Hand

Patience is required here, but this is really where things can get exciting. Hold the feeder in your lap and extend a finger as a perch. Stay as motionless as you can, and eventually, you might feel a hummingbird settle on your outstretched finger. Wait until no hummingbirds are present before you move your hand.

Think Tiny

Feeder designers know how beloved hummingbirds are, and that is why they created feeders that fit into your hand. Inexpensive miniature hand feeders can be purchased online or at local bird supply stores and work like a charm. You also can make one from a vial, a narrow glass jar or other small container. Wrap red ribbon around the top of a homemade feeder, then attach a plastic feeder "flower" to the top of your vial or bottle. Hummingbirds use those clues to know where to insert their bills.

Bait and Switch

It's easy enough to hold your hand feeder beside the usual nectar feeder. To speed things up, especially in ruby-throated hummingbird regions, remove the usual feeder—wait until no hummingbirds are present—and hold out your hand feeder in its place. Prop your arm on the back of a chair or a deck railing to make the wait more comfortable. If you get restless, stroll around your yard with the hand feeder, and when you see a hummingbird at a flower, hold out the feeder.

Don't Give Up

No luck at first? No worries—try troubleshooting. Sweeten the recipe to 1 part sugar to 3 parts water for love at first sip. (Later you can go back to 4 parts water.) Also, fill your hand feeder up to the brim, so there is very little effort required by the hummingbirds and they get instant payoff.

CLOSE ENCOUNTERS
A reader shares her story.

A few summers ago, I started spending 15 minutes each day standing as motionless as possible next to my hummingbird feeder. My visitors quickly got used to my presence. One hummingbird was bold enough to buzz around my head so close I could feel the wind from its wings against my hair.

My brother-in-law gave me a hand-held feeder for my birthday, and within five minutes or so a hummingbird was eating out of my hand! It moved back and forth between the feeders, seemingly in no hurry to leave. This is one birding experience that will stay with me for many years to come.

Lorraine Hoffman
GREENSBURG, PENNSYLVANIA

A ruby-throated finds himself drawn to red.

Think like a Hummingbird

Our experts have studied behavioral cues to tell you what's on a bird's mind.

HUMMINGBIRDS ARE SOME of the most fascinating and flashy fliers you'll ever see. Yet they're also some of the most misunderstood. If you want to attract these feathered friends and, better yet, make them regular visitors to your backyard, you've first got to understand what makes them tick. It takes a good bird behavioral expert to do that. Lucky, we've got the whole team at *Birds & Blooms* to guide you.

Our expert team has spent years studying hummingbird behaviors, habitats and feeding patterns to make educated assumptions about their likes and dislikes. Allow us to play mind reader. Here's what a hummingbird might say, if they could, on their next zoom past you.

A black-chinned and rufous hummingbird peacefully gather.

We'll flock to red.

In North America, the flowers best adapted for hummingbird pollination are bright red blooms with a tubular shape. Hummers instinctively watch for red things and investigate them. (We've seen them making detours to check out the taillights of parked cars and even someone's sunburned nose.) There's no question that planting red flowers will help to bring them to your yard.

We don't need fancy food.

Some companies sell hummingbird nectar, but you can easily make your own. Measure out 1 part white sugar to 4 parts water and mix thoroughly. If you boil the mixture to remove impurities, it may keep longer before it starts to spoil. And don't mix in any honey, red dye or other additives. Simple sugar and water work just fine.

Keep it clean, please.

Sugar water that has started to grow moldy can be dangerous to birds. It's essential that you keep feeders clean and replace the mixture regularly—at least once every three or four days, and more often in hot weather. If the mixture starts to look cloudy, clean the feeder and replace the nectar immediately.

Help us see the feeder.

Hummers are always looking around for food sources and they're good at finding them, but you can help by putting your feeder in a place that's easy to spot. Use a feeder with some bright red on it and position it where it can be seen by birds flying past at a distance.

Give us a little extra space.

Goldfinches and some other songbirds may feed together peacefully, but hummingbirds often

Juvenile or female
ruby-throated
hummingbird

Anna's hummingbirds (left) are common on the West Coast. Look closely and you might see their tiny nests (below left) perched on branches of shrubs and trees. An even lovelier sight: a mother with her young (below right).

fight around feeders, chasing one another away. Hummers are adapted to feeding at flowers, which will produce only limited amounts of nectar, so they instinctively protect their food sources even when they're at feeders with an unlimited supply. Try putting up two or more feeders that can't be seen from one another. Even the toughest little hummer can't monopolize multiple feeders if he or she can't see them all at once.

We're creatures of habit.

If the hummingbirds returning in spring seem to remember where you had flowers or feeders in previous years, they probably do. As tiny creatures that rely on specialized food sources in a big, big world, they have to be good at finding their way back to the best spots. They have a highly developed sense of what scientists call spatial memory. This is a good reason to work extra hard at attracting them. Once you get them established, they'll be back for more.

Rivoli's hummingbird

It's not you. It's me.

While the hummingbirds enjoy having your backyard as a nectar source, they aren't relying on you 100 percent. One of the top questions we're asked is: "If I have my feeder out in fall, will it keep the hummers from migrating?" The answer is no. They'll migrate when they're ready, whether or not feeders are available. It's instinct!

Leave it to the ladies.

Backyard birders sometimes worry because they had a pair of hummingbirds around and then the male disappeared, leaving a single mother behind. But this is normal for hummers. The male never helps with nest building,

incubation or feeding the young. The amazing mother hummingbird does all that work herself. Meanwhile, the male bird goes off in search of another female. It seems odd to humans, but this behavior ensures that there will be even more hummingbirds for us to enjoy.

Stay alert, but be patient.

It may take some time for hummers to find your feeder. And even after they do, it could be a while before you notice that they're visiting. They may zip in to the feeder for a quick sip many times before you happen to catch them in the act. So keep the feeder ready, and keep watching. You're likely to be rewarded.

CHAPTER 3

Create a Winning Hummingbird Habitat

Want frequent fliers? Your backyard can be aflutter with activity when you set the right scene. Enjoy the show!

Backyard Bliss for Humingbirds

A sustainable, safe space will attract your favorite flying jewels. Here's how to get started.

Ruby-throated hummingbird

BENEFITS IN EVERY CORNER
Plant garden containers with hummingbird favorites.

I F YOU LOVE HUMMINGBIRDS, there's a good chance you're already planting, growing and gardening with them in mind. But there's always a way to do more.

So how to best maximize your backyard space for these winged marvels? And how do you get more bang for your buck? We'll answer these questions and more.

Keep in mind that it can take years for garden spaces to reach their full potential, so don't let our list overwhelm you. But that doesn't mean you can't make a difference now. For starters, pick three things on this list to implement this year—or more, if you're feeling ambitious. The hummingbirds in your area will thank you.

Make a Dedicated Garden

That's right—create a space just for your flying friends. If you don't already have a designated hummingbird garden, now is the time to create one. You'll find entire books and websites dedicated to the subject, so consult some resources and get as creative as you like.

Expand your canvas with containers. Don't have the space to start a whole new garden? No problem! Containers are a stylish solution. Hanging baskets add flair and can offer a good source of nectar. You'll be amazed at some of the containers on the market, especially the self-watering ones.

Get rid of invasive plants. Start by going online to *plants.usda.gov* and click Introduced, Invasive and Noxious Plants on the left. You can search by state to see some invasive plants in your area. Once you know what they are, work to get them out as soon as possible.

Plant more natives. While you're ridding your yard of invasive plants, replace them with natives, which almost always suit the needs of local hummers. Planting native

plants, vines, shrubs and trees suited to your growing conditions will feed and shelter hummingbirds for many years to come.

Lose some grass. Most American backyards sport more grass than anything else. It might sound overwhelming to think about shrinking your lawn all at once—so don't! Put in a garden bed here and there in stages. Before you know it, you'll have a slew of new hummingbird-friendly plants and a lot less grass to mow.

Fortify the perimeter. Provide protective cover from predators and weather by planting shrubbery, especially around the perimeter of your yard. Creating safe boundaries also encourages hummingbirds to take up residence in your backyard, giving you the chance to see more of them.

Never underestimate the value of a good tree. If you plan it right, a good tree can offer many benefits to hummingbirds, including nectar in spring and nesting space in summer. Go ahead and invest in a new tree for your backyard. You won't be sorry.

An Anna's hummingbird
raises a pretty pair (left).
A bubbling bird bath
(below) is a major
attraction. A ruby-throat
(right) is lured to foxglove.

Attract the Hummingbirds

Put out a buffet. In addition to offering plants
rich in nectar, it's a good idea to offer sugar water.
Of course, the hummingbirds will do just fine
without it, but if you want an up-close view, this
is the way to get it. Opt for several sugar-water
feeders set far enough apart that hummers can't
see one another (although tiny, they can be very
territorial).

    Invite insects. Nectar isn't the only food
source to attract hummingbirds. Small insects,
which they catch in the air or on the leaves of
plants, provide the protein hummingbirds need
to maintain their busy bodies and grow new
feathers. In fact, young hummingbirds not
strong enough to fledge eat insects and spiders
almost exclusively. Eliminate insecticides to
keep the insect population healthy and thriving.

    Offer some water. Along with food and
shelter, water is one of the three necessities of
every backyard habitat. A larger water feature
is a smart addition and will attract a variety of
birds, but consider adding a shallow birdbath or
mister. Hummingbirds will flock to most water
sources, especially in the heat of summer.

    Reduce chemical use. When you have
hummingbirds exploring your backyard, the
last thing you want is for them to be harmed
by pesticides or herbicides. Make an effort to
reduce chemical use for the health of wildlife.

    Keep cats inside. Yes, it's a hard one for
all of the cat lovers out there, but even birding
experts who own cats agree with this one. Cats
are a leading cause of bird deaths, so it's best if
they stay inside.

SET THE TABLE
Black-eyed Susans (left) offer nectar to visitors. A male ruby-throated (right) visits a sugar-water feeder.

Don't Forget the Details

Show love to native plants. Bee balm, phlox and salvia are just a few of the native perennials that hummingbirds can't resist. To attract these jeweled fliers, remember that natives are always best.

Don't forget to offer lots of red. It's a proven fact: Hummingbirds love red. So be sure to plant enough red flowers to keep them coming back for more.

Choose spring-through-fall blooms. You don't want all your flowers to fade just when fall migration is starting. Plan carefully, picking flowers that hit their peak in various seasons, and you'll always have something to offer.

Be mindful of migration. Spring and late summer are big times for attracting hummingbirds. Even if you don't have regular summer visitors, don't give up.

Make sure your sugar-water feeders are filled. You don't want visitors to lose interest in your yard. Keep feeders full so the birds will stay around all summer. And be sure to change the sugar water regularly.

Keep the water coming. Hummingbirds especially love misters. They produce an ultra-fine water spray that hummers love to bathe in and drink from.

Think of the Big Picture

Set goals. Don't overdo it. Maybe your goal is to add a few hummingbird-friendly container plantings this year. Or maybe you have a more ambitious plan to start a whole new hummingbird garden. Whatever it is, no matter how big or small, it's important to set goals each season and then follow through.

Turn your yard into an experiment. Citizen science projects such as eBird, Backyard Bird Count, NestWatch and more are looking for birders and gardeners like you to provide valuable data for researchers. Sign up to help science for generations to come.

Get the whole family involved. Making your yard more hummingbird-friendly will be a lot more fun if you can involve everyone in your family. Have a discussion early on about why you're doing this and what it means. Then note things to watch for and assign individual jobs.

Share your success with the neighbors. Rethinking your backyard is an excellent first step, but involving others is when it really starts to make a difference. Let them know why you're reducing your lawn or putting up more sugar-water feeders. If you can get the whole neighborhood involved, you'll see results much faster.

Be a joiner. Join the Audubon Society, a nonprofit organization committed to creating bird-friendly communities. With expert advice and an extensive native plant database, it's a great resource to keep you on track. Learn more at *audubon.org*.

Certify your backyard. The National Wildlife Federation has one of the best-known programs with its Certified Wildlife Habitat, which lets you pledge to provide food, water and shelter in your yard. If you haven't yet certified your backyard (you probably already meet the requirements), now is the time. Go to *nwf.org* for more info.

High-Rise Hummingbirds

Tempt birds to your balcony with flashy flowers and a trio of tricks.

HUMMINGBIRDS FLY **FORWARD,** backward, sideways...and up, up, up! They go where the food is and to the colors they love most—red, orange and even rich pink. If you think about it, flowering trees, such as redbud, eucalyptus and mimosa, are nectar favorites, and they bloom far above the ground. Hummingbirds will go for it. They've even been spotted checking out the rooftop gardens of city high rises. So the sky really is the limit.

To make your way-above-ground offerings truly stand out, focus on vivid flowers. For a sunny balcony, geraniums are a solid choice. Their bloom clusters are huge and draw the eye of humans and hummingbirds alike from a distance. But geraniums are generally scanty in nectar, so make sure to add a pot or rail box of nectar-rich nasturtiums (long-blooming and easy to start from seed), New Guinea impatiens or other hummingbird-friendly flowers to keep the nectar-seekers there once they arrive. If your balcony is on the shady side, try annual shade impatiens (Impatiens walleriana). They offer a satisfying nectar source while beckoning from above ground.

Maybe your thumb isn't the greenest. Have no fear—you can always fake it! Wrap a length of red-flowered garland around your balcony rail, stick sprays of fake geraniums into a vase on a bistro table, or fill a railing window box with the brightest red and orange artificial flowers you can find.

Fake blooms work fine to attract a hummer's attention, but the birds won't stick around once they discover you've played a little trick. So make sure you're still giving them a sweet payoff. If you use artificial flowers to attract hungry birds, add mini nectar feeders on wire stems to your flowerpots. You should also make sure your full-size feeder is full of sugar water, and is close by and visible.

One last tip to get the most out of your high-rise hummingbird haven: Add perches. The tiny birds spend as much as 80 percent of their waking hours at rest. They prefer a relatively high perch with a clear view. So straighten out a wire coat hanger (it's the perfect diameter for those tiny feet), twist one end onto the railing and bend the top horizontally to provide a lookout. When the busy little birds have an inviting place to sit and rest between rounds of feeding, they're bound to linger a little longer.

TOP PICKS FOR CONTAINERS
Six bright blooms that hummingbirds can't resist.

- Petunia
- Verbena
- Salvia
- Lantana (above)
- Impatiens
- Penstemon

SMALL YET MIGHTY

Hummingbirds may not look it, but they are true powerhouses. Most North American species beat their wings between 50 and 100 times per second, and Anna's reach flying speeds of 60 miles per hour during courtship displays.

So Happy Together

Make your garden a place where both hummingbirds and butterflies can flutter around happily. No space is too small.

Female ruby-throated and monarch at butterfly bush.

Female black-chinned hummingbird

AS A LONGTIME SMALL-SPACE gardener, my motto has always been this: There's always room somewhere! And when that space could invite a few beautiful hummingbirds and butterflies your way, it's well worth the time to make it.

These beautiful flying friends add color and life to any size landscape, balcony or container garden. Here are my best tips for attracting hummingbirds and butterflies when you have limited space but a lot of love for nature.

Step 1: Add Flowers

Attract Hummingbirds. You can apply any small-space planting strategy, as long as you include nectar-rich flowers like nicotiana, fuchsia, nasturtiums, salvia and other hummingbird favorites. Don't be afraid to use perennials in containers. Columbine, hostas, honeysuckle vine and penstemons will return each year to guarantee meals for your visitors.

Beckon Those Butterflies. Many flowers that appeal to hummingbirds will appeal to butterflies, too, but the latter are especially drawn to verbena, zinnia, black-eyed Susans, marigolds, gayfeather and coneflower. And don't forget food for the caterpillars. Parsley, dill and fennel add striking color and texture to the garden, while also flavoring your dinner and feeding caterpillars. Though the insects do eat the leaves, there will still be plenty for you to enjoy. More good news: These plants recover quickly when the caterpillars finish feeding.

Step 2: Add More Flowers

Double Up on Plantings. Combine equally assertive plants for double the bloom or extended color in limited space. For instance, plant grape hyacinths in a ground cover of deadnettle to double the color in your late-spring or early-summer garden, enticing even more butterflies or hummingbirds. Two other options: Consider combining Blue Angel hostas and hakone grass together in a shady corner, or plant colchicum with bugleweed.

Go Vertical. Growing skyward lets you pack lots of nectar-rich flowers, habitat and food for the caterpillars in very little space. Think about vines, espaliered trees, shrubs in containers and green walls.

Add Containers. Try some hummingbird, butterfly and caterpillar favorites in containers. Grow them alone in individual pots, or mix them up. Annuals are always an easy pick, but perennials, as well as small-scale trees and shrubs, will also work in pots. For best results in colder climates, grow container plants one or two zones hardier than usual in a weatherproof pot.

BLOOMS BECKON

Get inspiration from a mix of phlox, petunias and butterfly flower (near right). A giant swallowtail and a white peacock share space at coneflowers. Grow hibiscus in containers to attract birds such as this female ruby-throat.

Extend Bloom Time. Increase the traffic by offering both early- and late-season bloomers. Add some cool-season annuals like pansies, stocks and snapdragons to your spring and fall garden. You might also consider growing native and ornamental grasses, which add motion and texture year-round. Many grasses provide nectar for butterflies, while the seeds feed a variety of birds and the whole plant can provide nesting material.

Step 3: Enjoy!

Put Out Resting Spots. Place a flat stone in your garden for butterflies to spread their wings and warm their bodies; they'll repay you with some perfect photo opportunities. For the hummingbird visitors, hang a perch near your sugar-water feeder.

Try Water Features. Add a puddle where the butterflies can gather and lap up a bit of moisture and salt. Sink a wide, shallow dish, flowerpot or bucket filled with sand into the soil. Keep it damp and wait for the party to begin. For hummingbirds, add a mister or some sort of slow-moving water feature. Make your own, or look for small-scale fountains or other water features at the garden center.

Plan a Great View. Be sure to place your containers and build your gardens where you can watch these charming guests feed on the plants. Consider the views from inside your home looking out. A hanging basket near a kitchen or family room window can bring butterflies and hummingbirds within view. Think about including sitting areas near the garden, or moving containers closer to your seating. Then wait for the show to begin.
—*Melinda Myers*

Container Combos

With blooming beauties like petunias, salvias and calibrachoas, your backyard becomes a popular hummingbird hot spot in no time. Get growing in a snap with these easy planting plans from Proven Winners.

Whether you have a sprawling landscape or a small patio, growing nectar-rich blooms in pots is a no-fail way to boost the hummingbird and butterfly population in your garden. These cherished fliers flock to colorful flowers that are nestled into favorite pots. The major benefit of this small-space strategy is placing the pots wherever you need to—near a sugar-water feeder, a shady corner or a sunny balcony. Try these two combos, or mix and match with other hummingbird favorites.

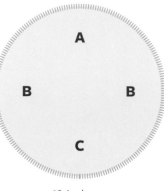

12-inch pot

A Ablazin' Purple Salvia
Quantity: 1

B Colorblaze Lime Time Coleus
Quantity: 2

C Superbells Evening Star Calibrachoa
Quantity: 2

THE DIRT ON DIRT

It's tempting to toss some dirt from the garden right into your containers, but a thoughtful potting mix that includes vermiculite, peat moss, compost, perlite or a combination of these materials yields the best results.

A   B

B   A

16-inch pot

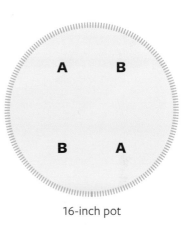

A Surfinia Sky Blue Petunia
Quantity: 2

B Supertunia Mini Rose Veined Petunia
Quantity: 2

Backyard Showers

Attract more hummingbirds to your space with moving water.

MOST BACKYARD BIRDS love to bathe and splash around in a clean birdbath—hummingbirds included! Although they occasionally stop at a shallow bath for a dip, these tiny birds prefer to wet their feathers by flying through or sitting under a gentle spray. One of the best ways to transform your landscape into a hummingbird hub is to incorporate a moving water feature.

Unlike other birds, hummingbirds want a light shower instead of a complete soak because their primary concern is simply to get their feathers clean. Most of their other hydration needs are met by all the sugar water and liquid flower nectar they slurp up.

Hummingbirds rinse off in the rain, at splashing streams or in the spray of waterfalls, and you can re-create the same kind of natural showers they love in your own backyard. It's easy!

To set up an inexpensive solar fountain, you'll need a basin deep enough to submerge a small pump or hold a floating model. The basin should be wide enough to catch and recycle the falling spray. A classic pedestal birdbath can work; its basin is usually both wide and deep. But because it may be too deep for hummingbirds, you should add stones if needed to keep the water shallow.

Maintenance is fairly simple, too. Make sure to keep an eye on the water level, especially on windy days. Refill the basin as needed to assure that the pump doesn't run dry.

The best thing about a solar fountain is that you don't need an electrical outlet, so you can put the birdbath almost anywhere. Just be sure that the small solar panel, attached by a cord to the pump, is in direct sunlight. The fountain will temporarily stop spraying on overcast days or if a large cloud moves across the sun.

Once you have a solar fountain bubbling away, it's time to amp things up. Add a tiny perch beside it so you can watch one of these busy birds for a few extra minutes as it stops to buzz its wings and contort its body to catch every drop of water.

NEAT AND TIDY

Clean water keeps hummingbirds coming back. Reader Lisa Swanson of Maricopa, Arizona, whose photos are featured here, has this advice: "I disassemble my fountain and use a brush and warm water to clean it every two to three days, then refill it with fresh water."

To make a resting spot, choose a slim branching stick (about 4 feet long) with twigs skinny enough for tiny feet to easily grasp. Dead, twiggy branches that fall from maples and other deciduous trees make ideal perches. Push the bottom of the stick into the soil beside the basin to anchor it. It's even better if part of the branch extends through the spray, so hummingbirds can have a spot right in the droplets.

Then just sit back and enjoy some special moments of watching zipping, preening hummingbirds in your backyard showers.

Rufous
hummingbird

Money-Saving Secrets

Here's how to keep costs down while still getting major payoff in the hummingbird-sighting department.

EVEN IF YOU HAVEN'T had luck attracting hummingbirds this summer, don't give up. Juveniles will be looking for a place to eat, and you could attract visitors at any time. Meanwhile, keep your costs down with these tips.

Use your leftovers. Overripe cantaloupe? Put it out for the hummingbirds. They'll devour it instead of it going to waste.

Remember your successes. If you've had a lot of luck luring hummers with cannas or bee balm, stick with them. Don't waste money on other plants that won't work as well.

Go red! While flowers are ideal, just about anything that's red will interest hummingbirds. Attach leftover ribbons, bows, pieces of an old scarf or even artificial flowers to your feeder.

Make your sugar water. Remember, all it takes is 4 parts water to 1 part sugar. Boil it, cool it and voila! No need for store-bought nectar. Skip the red food coloring, too. It's not necessary.

Be patient and relax. The best bargain is a seat in your yard. Enjoy the sights and sounds of the garden—and, with luck, the hummingbirds!

Choose wisely. If you place your feeders in the shade, you'll get less algae growth, so you won't have to change the sugar water nearly as often.

Double up. Save time and money by giving your old toothbrush a purposeful new life: Use it to scrub those hard-to-reach parts of your hummingbird feeder.

Attract nesters. Go ahead and let your dandelions go to seed. The hummingbirds will use the seeds to line their nests.

Don't get fancy. Anything that holds water can be made into a working feeder. If it's red, that's even better. So make your own, or just stick with inexpensive, basic feeders. The hummers won't care.

Large firecracker plant

READER TIPS
Here are ideas from some active hummingbird devotees.

Hummingbirds don't like to wait for their food while I wash their sugar-water feeder, so I hang a spare one while I'm busy cleaning.

Judy Talbott
ROCHESTER, INDIANA

Wasps are pests at hummingbird feeders. I've solved the problem with cooking oil. Each time I clean out my feeder, I dip my finger in oil and rub it around the feeding ports. No more wasps.

Betty Rochester
PINE BLUFF, ARKANSAS

My children and I learned that if we rest our fingers on the perches of our hummingbird feeders, the birds will readily perch on them as they drink the sugar water. The experience is amazing.

Debbie Eberting
CLINTON, MISSOURI

We have a small pond in our backyard with a waterfall that produces a light mist. The hummingbirds love to whiz through the mist and drink the pond.

Helen Miller EVANT, TEXAS

I plant peas on trellises between my feeders. This seems to deter hummingbirds from claiming feeders and bullying others, because it prevents visual contact among the birds. Plus, the pea blossoms provide an additional nectar source.

Jim Low JEFFERSON CITY, MISSOURI

CHAPTER 4

Best Plant Picks

Grow a garden that attracts flying friends. Try nectar-rich annuals, perennials and vines. From easy-grow natives to pretty patio stunners, these are the top picks.

❮ Agastache

AGASTACHE SPP., ZONES 4 TO 11
☀

Bushy and studded with blooms from mid- to late summer, agastache is a favorite of hummingbirds, butterflies and bees. Flower spires in violet, orange, yellow, pink or blue reach 2 to 6 feet high. Agastache thrives in full sun and in well-draining, fertile soil.

⌃ Aster

ASTER OR SYMPHYOTRICHUM SPP., ZONES 3 TO 10
⛅ ☀

Asters bear daisylike flowers that crowd the top of the stems, like those of New England aster, or branch out to the sides like the calico aster. Many bloom during hummingbird migration in late summer and fall. Asters usually like moist soil and plentiful sun. Late season butterflies also love asters, especially when mixed with other plants, such as ironweed and goldenrod.

⌃ Autumn Sage

SALVIA GREGGII, ZONES 6 TO 10
⛅ ☀

Catch migrating hummingbirds with reddish shades of salvia. The annual of this plant (*S. splendens*) has always been a good choice for those flying jewels, so now try adding the perennial version to your garden. Grow this impressive 2- to 3-foot-tall native Texan shrub in a sunny spot in well-drained soil. Want another color? Autumn sage is also available in orange, purple, white and more.

❮ Bee Balm

MONARDA SPP., ZONES 3 TO 9
☀

Also known as bergamot, this unusual beauty grows up to 4 feet tall and starts flowering in midsummer, inviting visiting hummingbirds, butterflies and bees to your flower bed. Plants come in hues of pink, red, white and purple. Choose mildew resistant varieties for best results. Frequent deadheading keeps this enthusiastic self-sower in check, but then you won't see songbirds stopping to eat the seeds once the petals die back. The choice is yours!

⌃ Butterfly Bush

BUDDLEJA DAVIDII, ZONES 5 TO 9

☀

A top nectar plant for many winged species, drought and heat tolerant butterfly bush grows up to 15 feet tall. Arching branches are tipped with tiny purple, white, pink or yellow blooms from midsummer through frost. While invasive in some areas, noninvasive species are available.

⌃ Butterfly Weed

ASCLEPIAS TUBEROSA, ZONES 3 TO 9

☀

Not solely a treat for butterflies, this drought tolerant plant is a wildlife garden must-have if it's hummingbirds you're after. They love the flat-topped flower clusters' nectar, and birds like goldfinches and orioles use the silky down of spent seed pods as nesting material. Despite its name, it's far from being a pest.

❭ Buttonbush

CEPHALANTHUS OCCIDENTALIS, ZONES 5 TO 10

☁☀

Round white flower heads with needlelike protrusions make buttonbush unmistakable. But it's the honey-sweet nectar that brings the hummingbirds in. Shrubs are generally about 6 feet tall but occasionally far surpass that. Consistently moist soil is a must; downright wet soil, a plus.

❭ Calibrachoa

CALIBRACHOA SPP., ANNUAL TO ZONE 9

☀

Small flowers like petunias steal the show all season, making fast-growing calibrachoa a hot choice for beds and containers—especially those that are geared towards hummingbirds. Use it as a nicely textured filler plant or as a bold stand-alone. Plants reach about 8 inches tall and spread to about 1 foot wide.

❮ Canary Creeper

TROPAEOLUM PEREGRINUM,
ANNUAL TO ZONE 9
☀️

Take a close look at the bright yellow flowers and you'll see the inspiration for the common name. Grow this climbing nasturtium in full sun to part shade with moist, well-draining soil. Train it on a trellis, grow it in a hanging basket or allow it to scramble through other plants.

⌃ Candy Corn Plant

MANETTIA LUTEORUBRA,
ANNUAL TO ZONE 10
⛅

This noncaloric candy corn is fun for gardeners of all ages. The orange tubular flowers that beckon hummingbirds are tipped in yellow, making them look like the Halloween treat. Grow it in light shade and moist, well-draining soil.

⌃ Cardinal Flower

LOBELIA CARDINALIS, ZONES 3 TO 9
⛅ ☀️

A moisture-loving favorite, bright red cardinal flower grows 3 to 5 feet tall and blooms for most of summer and into autumn. It does well when planted in full sun to partial shade and fertile, moist soil. Hummingbirds and butterflies seek out this plant's nectar, but don't expect to see cardinals hanging around nearby—the flower is named merely for the color.

❮ Carolina Silverbell

HALESIA TETRAPTERA
(OR *HALESIA CAROLINA*),
ZONES 4 TO 8
⛅ ☀️

This North American native tree is as low-maintenance as its blooms are beautiful. Hummingbirds adore this showy spring stunner and its snowy white bell-shaped blooms in late April to early May. It grows 30 to 40 feet tall and 20 to 35 feet wide, and does best in acidic soil. Pair it with another hummer favorite like rhododendrons or azaleas.

❮ Walker's Low Catmint

NEPETA RACEMOSA 'WALKER'S LOW', ZONES 4 TO 9

☁ ⛅ ☀

Beautiful, reliable Walker's Low Catmint creates a 2 to 3 foot mound of flowers from May to November. Give it a haircut to slow down the blooms and fix floppy growth. Just cut about halfway down the stem.

︿ Cigar Flower

CUPHEA IGNEA, ANNUAL TO ZONE 10

☀

This plant is one of the gardening world's best-kept secrets, enticing hummingbirds with long tubular blooms that shine from spring through autumn. Once you see the results you get, it'll become a staple in your garden every year.

︿ Columbine

AQUILEGIA SPP., ZONES 3 TO 9

☁ ⛅ ☀

Blooming exuberantly from spring to early summer, columbine's distinctive flowers come in a wide spectrum of solids and bicolors, with single or double sets of petals. Plants range from 8 inches to 3 feet high. Watch for other pollinators, such as the duskywing butterfly, which uses this as a host plant.

❮ Cleome

CLEOME HASSLERIANA, ANNUAL TO ZONES 8

⛅ ☀

Plant this tropical native in your garden and you're sure to attract attention. This bloom, which some call spider flower, is a top nectar source for hummingbirds. Cleome's tall stems, topped by wispy pink, purple or white flowers, are hard to miss. Plants tend to reseed themselves from one year to the next if goldfinches don't get to them first!

❮ Common Bugleweed

AJUGA REPTANS, ZONES 3 TO 9

☁ ⛅ ☀

This evergreen perennial makes an excellent ground cover with its masses of bronze, green or variegated foliage. Columns of blue or pink flowers appear in spring and early summer, inviting butterflies and hummingbirds. An aggressive grower that may invade lawns, it's best planted within a barrier. On the upside, you won't have to wait long for it to fill in after planting!

^ Coneflower

ECHINACEA SPP.,
ZONES 3 TO 9

☀

Though its flowers are not tube-shaped, this easy-grow plant is still a hummingbird favorite for its nectar, as well as the tiny insects it attracts. You'll also see songbirds pause to nibble the seeds in fall. In winter, seed heads that remain provide interesting garden focal points.

^ Coral Bells

HEUCHERA SANGUINEA, ZONES 3 TO 8

☁ ⛅ ☀

Wands of primarily red bell-shaped flowers and handsome, sometimes evergreen, foliage make this bloomer a valuable addition to any garden, whether it's located in a sunny or shady spot. This adaptable mounding plant is a striking border or container plant and will increase hummingbird traffic in your yard. To extend coral bells' blooming season, clip off spent stems

❮ Crape Myrtle

LAGERSTROEMIA INDICA,
ZONES 7 TO 9

☀

Crape myrtle is a year-round belle in the South, where it thrives in the warmth and blooms from July to September. The spectacular flowers won't stop attracting butterflies, bees and hummingbirds. You can even remove the first wave of flowers to encourage a second bloom. Grow this heat tolerant beauty in full sun and it might get to be 10 feet or more.

⌃ Crocosmia

CROCOSMIA SPP., ZONES 5 TO 9

☀

This dramatic hummingbird magnet reaches 3 feet high, unfurling wiry stems of bright blossoms from mid- to late summer. Moist soil is important for optimal flowering. Crocosmia makes an excellent cut flower and adds tropical flair to both outdoor and indoor spaces. But be warned: It's invasive in some areas.

⌃ Cup and Saucer Vine

COBAEA SCANDENS, ANNUAL TO ZONE 9

☀

This vine is a vigorous grower, so give it a sturdy support to climb and display its cup-shaped, aromatic flowers. The blooms open green and then mature to purple, lasting about four days. Grow in full sun and provide a bit of shade in the afternoon in hotter regions.

❯ Dahlia

DAHLIA SPP., ZONES 8 TO 11

☀

It's no wonder the dahlia is the darling of many gardeners. With thousands of cultivars, there is a color, shape and size for everyone. Some varieties easily surpass 5 feet, and the flowers grow as big as dinner plates. Gardeners in cooler climates should dig up the tubers once the plants have died back after frost arrives.

❯ Daylily

HEMEROCALLIS, ZONES 3 TO 10

☁ ☀

This summer bloomer is cherished for its reliability and variety. With many thousands of cultivars available, gardeners have almost limitless options. Some are even named after their fast-flying admirers, such as the Dixie Hummingbird cultivar. Though the blossoms last just a day, you'll find many hybrids that flower repeatedly all season long.

‹ Delphinium

DELPHINIUM, ZONES 3 TO 7

This towering treasure makes a statement as a vertical accent at the back of a mixed border or in a container. Dozens of blooms on each stem give hummingbirds plenty of nectar sources to share with butterflies and other bugs.

⌃ Evening Primrose

OENOTHERA, ZONES 3 TO 9

A good choice for poor or dry soil, warm tones of this spring to summer bloomer attract hummers best. Typically, plants reach heights of 2 to 3 feet and may need support.

⌃ Figwort

ASARINA SCANDENS, ANNUAL TO ZONE 9

Brighten the summer and fall garden with the indigo, violet, pink or white flowers of figwort. Grow it in full sun to part shade on a trellis or allow the trailing stems to spill over the edge of a hanging basket.

‹ Flowering Crabapple

MALUS, ZONES 4 TO 8

Crabapples are the darlings of late spring. Flowers of white, pink or deep crimson beckon hummingbirds before transforming into dainty fruits in yellow, orange, maroon or red. Select a newer variety to ensure good resistance to disease and pests, and make sure you allow enough space, as some can grow 20 to 25 feet tall and wide.

︿ Flowering Tobacco

NICOTIANA SPP., ANNUAL TO ZONE 10

For a no-fuss way to liven up your garden, plant flowering tobacco! Ranging from 10 inches to 5 feet high, the stems are covered with star-shaped flowers in shades of red, maroon, lavender, white, pink, yellow and even green. Some types, including members of the *N. sylvestris* species, have a lovely scent, especially in the evening.

︿ Four-O'Clocks

MIRABILIS JALAPA, ANNUAL TO ZONE 10

Almost like clockwork, this often fragrant flower blooms in late afternoon. Each blossom lives for just one day, fading before noon. Flowers are available in yellow, pink, purple, red, white and lavender—sometimes on the same plant. Additional varieties like the Jingles mix are striped.

❭ Foxglove

DIGITALIS SPP., ZONES 3 TO 10

With 18-inch to 6-foot spires covered with bright, bell-shaped blooms, this showy plant can't be missed. Self-seeding foxglove is a biennial or a short-lived perennial, so leave the spent flowers in place and you'll be treated to a new crop of blooms each spring.

❭ Fringed Bleeding Heart

DICENTRA EXIMIA, ZONES 3 TO 9

You may be surprised to learn this landscape plant is native to the eastern U.S. It blooms later than the larger common bleeding heart, which is native to Asia. The rosy to purplish red flowers appear in late spring and continue through midsummer on 12- to 18-inch plants. Grow fringed bleeding heart in partial shade and moist soil for best results.

‹ Fuchsia

FUCHSIA SPP., ANNUAL TO ZONE 8

Fuchsia's showy, pendulous red, white, pink and purple blooms will capture your heart. There are more than 100 kinds, from low-growing dwarfs and trailing plants to upright shrubs. Fuchsia grows best in moist soil and partial shade, so it's ideal for attracting hummingbirds to less-than-sunny yards. Fertilize weekly for the most vibrant results.

⌃ Geranium

PELARGONIUM

It's up for debate, but the geranium may be known and loved by more people than any other flower in the world. The plant's vivid colors and long-lasting blooms make it a favorite for backyards everywhere, flowering from summer to frost. Multicolored Peppermint Twist is eye-catching. The Orbit series has a glowing red variety that hummingbirds are sure to love.

⌃ Hollyhock

ALCEA ROSEA, ZONES 3 TO 9

If you want to make an impact in your garden, look no further than this old-fashioned favorite. It comes in many colors, attracts a variety of insects and hummingbirds, and can reach up to 8 feet tall. Hollyhock is a biennial, so it grows foliage on short stems its first year but doesn't flower until the next. From then on, it self-seeds.

‹ Hibiscus

HIBISCUS SPP., ZONES 5 TO 11

Beautiful and impressive, this exotic-looking shrub grows up to 15 feet tall. Its flowers span as wide as 12 inches, beckoning fliers of all types, and last from early summer until the first frost. Plant this stunner in rich, moist soil in a sunny site.

∧ Hyacinth Bean Vine

DOLICHOS LABLAB,
ANNUAL TO ZONE 10
☀

This purple beauty will quickly cover a trellis or fence, providing season-long color with its green leaves, fragrant white, pink or purple-pink flowers, and purple pods. Grow hyacinth bean in full sun to partial shade. Despite being an annual, it will often reseed in the garden.

∧ Impatiens

IMPATIENS SPP., ANNUAL TO ZONE 8
☁ ⛅ ☀

Invite winged creatures into the garden with impatiens. Sparrows, finches, grosbeaks and buntings eat the seeds, while hummingbirds and butterflies drop in for a sip of nectar. Growing 6 inches to 2 feet high, impatiens has a mounding growth habit, making it a good choice for borders, foundation beds and containers.

❯ Jupiter's Beard

CENTRANTHUS RUBER,
ZONES 5 TO 8
☀

Hummingbirds love hot pink blooms, and this sprawling perennial keeps pumping out clusters of tiny bright flowers from summer through very late fall. Snip off the fluffy seed head clusters to keep it blooming.

❯ Lantana

LANTANA CAMARA,
ANNUAL TO ZONE 9
☀

With lantana's abundant clusters of tiny nectar-rich flowers, why wouldn't hummingbirds love it? Later in the growing season, other birds nibble its berries. In more tropical climates, lantana is grown as a shrub and can become invasive. With their mounding or trailing habits, smaller varieties work well in containers.

❮ Lilac
SYRINGA SPP., ZONES 3 TO 8

Among spring's most anticipated sights and scents, the lilac attracts both hummingbirds and butterflies, and it serves as a nesting site for songbirds. A deciduous shrub growing up to about 20 feet tall and wide, this sun lover is at its best in small groups or as a specimen plant.

⌃ Lavender
LAVANDULA SPP., ZONES 5 TO 10

In the summertime, hummingbirds and other pollinators frequently visit lavender. You'll love this Mediterranean bloomer for its attractive flower spires, silvery green foliage and calming scent. Varieties of this flower grow from 1 to 4 feet tall and are available in many shades of purple as well as white and light pink.

⌃ Lupine
LUPINUS SPP., ZONES 3 TO 8

Give your backyard a bit of rustic charm by planting a stand of lupines. With colors and sizes that suit any garden, varieties range from native species to new hybrids. Hummingbirds, butterflies and songbirds all seek out this late-spring bloomer, which prefers sun or partial shade.

❮ Lungwort
PULMONARIA SPP., ZONES 2 TO 8

A popular early nectar source for hummingbirds, the blue, purple, pink or white blooms of lungwort and its dappled leaves lend interest to shady backyards. The intriguing foliage often remains green clear into winter, making this plant an all-season asset. Most cultivars grow about 12 inches tall and thrive in moist, well-draining soil.

⌃ Mexican Bush Sage

SALVIA LEUCANTHA, ANNUAL TO ZONE 8
☀

Hummingbirds and butterflies will clamor for a space at this plant's late-blooming purplish flowers. In areas where this sage is hardy, it can be established as a shrub. In cooler zones, plant it outdoors as soon as the threat of frost has passed, as it needs a long growing season. No matter where you live, grow Mexican bush sage in moist yet well-draining soil.

❯ Mandevilla

MANDEVILLA, ANNUAL TO ZONE 10
☁ ☀

A drought tolerant vine that can be grown in a container, hanging basket or right in the garden, mandevilla's trumpet-shaped blooms are what brings in the hummers. Look around and you'll find many new cultivars with white, pink, maroon, crimson or bicolor flowers.

⌃ Maltese Cross

LYCHNIS CHALCEDONICA, ZONES 3 TO 9
☀

With bold red flowers on a plant 2 to 3 feet high and 1 to 2 feet wide, this bright bloomer will dress up your summer flower garden and attract hummingbirds in a hurry. Plant it in fertile, moist, well-draining soil.

❯ Morning Glory

IPOMOEA SPP., ANNUAL TO ZONE 9
☀

A hummingbird favorite, the tubular flowers on this popular vine awake and open each morning to greet the day. Plants climb up to 12 feet high. Cultivars Grandpa Ott and Heavenly Blue are surefire glorious choices.

NASTURTIUM: ALL-AMERICA SELECTIONS; PENSTEMON: BAILEY NURSERIES
PASSIONFLOWER: RON NEWHOUSE; PETUNIA: COURTESY OF PROVEN WINNERS - WWW.PROVENWINNERS.COM

⌃ Passionflower

PASSIFLORA SPP., ZONES 5 TO 9

🌥 ☀

This quirky flower doesn't just look cool, it's a big draw for southern wildlife. Nectar-seekers visit its exotic-looking blossoms, while certain types of butterflies use the vine as a host. The fragrant flowers come in shades of purple, blue, red, pink, yellow and white. Vines range in length from 15 to 50 feet—most gardeners let the tendrils climb walls and fences, but others use it as a ground cover.

❮ Nasturtium

TROPAEOLUM SPP., ANNUAL TO ZONE 9

🌥 ☀

Humans aren't the only ones who enjoy nasturtiums. The nectar attracts many types of hungry fliers! Once established, nasturtium performs best when left alone, contributing vivid color all season long. Some types grow in mounds; others are good climbers.

⌃ Penstemon

PENSTEMON SPP., ZONES 3 TO 10

🌥 ☀

Hummingbirds favor this spiky trumpet-shaped flower, which comes in pink, red, purple, blue and white. Varieties reach heights of up to 4 feet and bloom profusely for most or all of the summer. Full sun and well-draining soil are ideal.

❮ Petunia

PETUNIA HYBRIDS, ANNUAL

🌥 ☀

All summer gardens should have a few easygoing petunias to fill the sunny spots. They're available in a wide range of colors and patterns, some featuring impressive stripes and bicolored blooms. Cut petunias back in summer if they become leggy for improved flowering. Petunias absolutely shine trailing from hanging baskets and bring visiting hummers up to eye level.

⌃ Phlox

PHLOX, ZONES 3 TO 9
☀

Butterflies crave it, hummingbirds can't resist it. After all, it smells delicious, the flowers are gorgeous—the list goes on and on. For upright phlox cultivars (garden phlox), choose disease resistant Tiara or David. For a more sprawling ground cover and early bloomer, try creeping phlox.

⌃ Pineapple Sage

SALVIA ELEGANS, ANNUAL TO ZONE 8
☀

Another annual in the salvia family, this sage is fairly new to the market. Proven Winners introduced this cultivar, Golden Delicious, which boasts lovely yellow foliage and bright red (hummingbirds' favorite color) blooms. It does very well in the heat, and it's a champ in containers.

❯ Pinkshell Azalea

RHODODENDRON VASEYI, ZONES 4 TO 7
☁ ☀

Brighten a partly shady woodland garden with the sweet blossoms of pinkshell azalea. This spring- and summer-blooming shrub attracts nectar-seeking fliers. Plant in a spot with plenty of room because it can reach up to 15 feet tall. Despite the name, some varieties bloom in white.

❯ Pinkroot

SPIGELIA MARILANDICA, ZONES 5 TO 9
☁ ☁

Hummers will be especially grateful when you add pinkroot to your garden. A rugged and handsome wildflower of modest size—from 1 to 2 feet tall and wide—it blooms from late spring to early summer. The spiky tube-shaped flowers are bright pink and yellow.

❮ Red Buckeye

AESCULUS PAVIA, ZONES 4 TO 8

⛅

In late spring, red buckeye unfurls 6-inch-long upright panicles of tubular red flowers that hummers can't resist. It grows to just 15 feet tall and 10 feet wide, so one of these would look right at home in most backyards. Moist, well-draining soil and partial shade provide the ideal growing conditions for this compact flowering tree.

⌃ Red-Hot Poker

KNIPHOFIA SPP., ZONES 4 TO 9

☀

Terrific in mixed flower borders and small groupings, torchlike red-hot poker plants grow up to 4 feet high with bright plumes of orange, red, yellow, white and green. For best results, well-draining soil is important; otherwise, the roots will rot in boggy conditions. Nectar-feeding hummingbirds and swallowtail butterflies love it.

⌃ Redbud

CERCIS SPP., ZONES 4 TO 9

⛅ ☀

An early-spring showstopper, this tree bursts with a profusion of purple, red, pink or white blossoms before the leaves emerge. Redbud's blooms attract hummers, butterflies and other pollinators. Plant yours where there's plenty of space, because they're often wider than they are tall.

❮ Rose of Sharon

HIBISCUS SYRIACUS, ZONES 5 TO 9

⛅

When other flowers are spent, this late bloomer becomes a generous source of energy for hummingbirds. A member of the hibiscus family, it bears charming trumpet-shaped flowers that bloom from late summer through midautumn. In optimal conditions, including moist, well-draining soil and lots of sunshine, it can climb to 10 feet or more.

⌃ Salvia

SALVIA SPLENDENS,
ANNUAL TO ZONE 10

☁ ☀

Also known as firecracker plant, this annual variety of salvia pops in any garden, producing season-long color in just about any landscape. Depending on the cultivar, this annual will reach 8 inches to 2 feet, though newer varieties are more compact.

⌃ Scarlet Gilia

IPOMOPSIS RUBRA, ZONES 5 TO 9

☀

Watch this plant transform from a mat of feathery foliage the first year to tall stems with finely dissected leaves and tubular red flowers the second year. Also known as standing cypress or Texas plume, gilia thrives in well-draining to dry soil.

❯ Scarlet Runner Bean

PHASEOLUS COCCINEUS,
ANNUAL TO ZONE 7

☀

Grow scarlet runner bean, a true favorite, in a sunny spot in your vegetable or flower garden. You can grow these long vines on a trellis, arbor or fence. Regular harvesting keeps the plant producing more pods and its beautiful scarlet flowers blossoming.

❯ Summersweet

CLETHRA ALNIFOLIA, ZONES 3 TO 9

☁ ☀

Native to the eastern states, fragrant summersweet is a pretty addition to any site. Spikes bearing bell-shaped pink or white blooms emerge in late summer, just in time to entice southbound fliers. Summersweet reaches 8 feet tall. If you have a small space, try Hummingbird—it's 2 to 3 feet tall.

❮ Trumpet Honeysuckle

LONICERA SEMPERVIRENS, ZONES 4 TO 9

☁️☀️

Plant this and you won't be the only one to fall for its elegant blossoms—hummingbirds are suckers for trumpet honeysuckle, too. Vines with red, orange and yellow blossoms climb up to 20 feet. Once the blooms of this North American native fade, songbirds will stop by to nibble the berries.

⌃ Trumpet Vine

CAMPSIS RADICANS ZONES 4 TO 9

☀️

There's a reason you see so many photos of hummingbirds at trumpet vines. They love this sweet beauty! A perennial classic, showy trumpet vine grows up to 40 feet, easily filling a trellis with its orange-red or yellow blooms. Prune it in spring and fall to keep it non-invasive.

⌃ Verbena

VERBENA X HYBRIDA, ANNUAL TO ZONE 9

☀️

Expect summerlong color from these attractive blooms that sit high above the plant's foliage, allowing hummingbirds easy access to the sweet nectar inside. The plant's stems spread out to about 18 inches. Keep the soil moist but well-drained for optimal flowering.

❮ Viburnum

VIBURNUM, ZONES 2 TO 9

☁️☀️

Every good plant list needs a shrub on it, and these are some of the most versatile, resilient and wildlife-friendly ones available. They have flowers in spring and summer, great foliage in fall and berries from fall to winter.

⌃ Weigela

WEIGELA SPP., ZONES 3 TO 9

☀

In addition to its pretty, trumpet-shaped late-spring flowers that entice returning hummingbirds, weigela boasts attractive foliage throughout the growing season. In some varieties, leaves change color in fall. Sizes range from about 2 to 8 feet tall and wide.

⌃ Wisteria

WISTERIA FLORIBUNDA, ZONES 5 TO 9

☀

There's nothing quite like a blooming garland of wisteria to add romance to a spring backyard, especially when the hummingbirds and butterflies arrive. Provide ample support for the vine's heavy, woody limbs, which can extend to more than 30 feet. Always prune wisteria each year after it flowers.

❯ Yucca

YUCCA FILAMENTOSA, ZONES 4 TO 11

☀

Many gardeners, especially those in the Southwest, enjoy yucca. It's about as drought tolerant as they come. Spiky evergreen leaves create a mound that's so substantial that birds nest within it, while hummingbirds crave the nectar from its beautiful columnar white flowers. It can reach 3 to 12 feet tall when in bloom.

❯ Zinnia

ZINNIA, ZONES 3 TO 10

☀

Nectar-filled zinnias come in a broad range of colors, heights and flower sizes, and they are a cheerful addition to backyards. Incredibly simple to start from seed, sun-loving zinnias bloom rather quickly. Seek out mildew resistant varieties if mildew disease is a problem in your area. A hummingbird and butterfly favorite, this versatile plant's seed heads attract several varieties of sparrows, finches and juncos.

CHAPTER 5

Beyond the Backyard

There's a whole wide world out there, full of hummingbirds and watching opportunities. From scenic day trips to full-on festivals, here are unique ways to enjoy our flying jewels.

Amazing Havens

Pack your bags—and don't forget to grab your binoculars.
These hummingbird hot spots are worth the trip.

Desert National Wildlife Refuge

LAS VEGAS, NEVADA

Bandelier National Monument
LOS ALAMOS,
NEW MEXICO

Davis Mountains
State Park
FORT DAVIS, TEXAS

THE WEST IS BEST when it comes to hummingbirds. Variations in terrain and rainfall create diverse habitats that attract up to 17 species.

Desert National Wildlife Refuge
LAS VEGAS, NEVADA

While the Mojave Desert is certainly hot, it's also an extraordinary spot for hummingbirds. This 1.6-million-acre wildlife refuge, the largest outside of Alaska, attracts 320 species of birds, including a number of hummingbird species—more than any other birding destination in Nevada.

Watch for: Costa's hummingbirds, which thrive in arid climates, and nest in the refuge during late winter and early spring. Anna's and black-chinned also flit among the sagebrush and wetland habitats at the refuge.

Do it: Birders flock to the Corn Creek visitor center, where the vegetation attracts many migrant and vagrant hummingbirds. Several trails begin here, some accessible to all, for the best hummingbird-watching.

Bandelier National Monument
LOS ALAMOS, NEW MEXICO

The Ancestral Pueblo people lived on the Pajarito Plateau in northern New Mexico until the mid-1500s, carving their homes into the volcanic tuff and farming atop the mesas in what is now Bandelier National Monument, a 33,000-acre park. It's a favorite destination among birding enthusiasts aiming to see not only hummingbirds but a wide diversity of birds more typical of western mountains, canyons and grasslands.

Watch for: Broad-tailed and black-chinned hummingbirds raise families in Bandelier National Monument. Calliope and rufous hummingbirds flit among the monument's cliffs, valleys and streams.

Do it: Celebrate the Year of the Bird, which comes in honor of the 100-year anniversary of the Migratory Bird Treaty Act. Naturalists will focus on a different bird each month, including broad-tailed hummingbirds in April.

Davis Mountains State Park
FORT DAVIS, TEXAS

Located in westernmost Texas, the Davis Mountains are hummingbird heaven from July to October. With high elevation (5,000 feet) and levels of precipitation, the range is one of the Southwest's sky island environments, making it a mecca for birds and other wildlife. Most hummingbird species in the U.S. have been spotted here.

Watch for: Broad-tailed, black-chinned and rufous hummingbirds are common, but don't be surprised if lucifer, ruby-throated or Calliope hummers whiz by. Ornithologists found the first-ever amethyst-throated hummingbird in the U.S. here. Nearby McDonald Observatory and the Nature Conservancy Davis Mountains Preserve maintain bird-viewing stations.

Do it: During the annual Davis Mountains Hummingbird Celebration, typically held every August, designated viewing spots in the park and in adjacent sanctuaries put you at the hummingbird hub, even on rainy days. Or join a workshop on how to garden for or properly feed these feisty sky-fairies.

Violet-crowned hummingbird

Ramsey Canyon Preserve
HEREFORD, ARIZONA

Anna's hummingbird

Cabrillo National Monument
SAN DIEGO, CALIFORNIA

Ramsey Canyon Preserve

HEREFORD, ARIZONA

The Huachuca Mountains, home to Ramsey Canyon Preserve, rise from the desert of southeastern Arizona and catch cooler air that creates both arid and subtropical microclimates in close proximity. As a result, the preserve is remarkably biodiverse, playing host to numerous hummingbird species.

Watch for: Ramsey Canyon attracts 15 species of hummingbirds, some of which only migrate this far north. It's a known hot spot for violet-crowned and berylline hummingbirds.

Do it: The Nature Conservancy offers guided walks from March through November, with April through September being the best time for bird-watching.

Cabrillo National Monument

SAN DIEGO, CALIFORNIA

Cabrillo National Monument, a seaside preserve surrounded by urban sprawl, is an oasis for birds and other marine and terrestrial wildlife. The monument has both residential and migratory hummingbirds.

Watch for: During mating season, male Anna's hummingbirds perform aerial acrobatics to attract a mate. Numerous coastal species winter here or migrate through, including Allen's, rufous, black-chinned and Costa's hummingbirds. In April, watch Calliope hummingbirds gather around the blooming bottlebrush trees.

Do it: Rangers offer guided tours and other activities daily. In addition to birding, they'll help you explore the tidal pools and watch for whales. Kids can pick up a Junior Ranger activity book at the visitor center to record the hummingbirds they see along the 2½-mile Bayside Trail and elsewhere in the park.

Home to about 15 hummingbird species, America's Southwest is the place to go if you're on a quest to see these winged wonders. While you're sure to see the regulars that stay all summer, spring and fall migration are the best times to see lesser-known species.

Anna's hummingbird feeding on a cactus bloom at Desert Botanical Garden in Phoenix, Arizona

Tohono Chul Park

Yosemite National Park

CALIFORNIA

In the Sierra Nevada Mountains, Calliope hummingbirds nest in the pine trees and sip nectar from the Indian paintbrush, columbine and larkspur that thrive in Yosemite's meadows and forests. This national park also provides a year-round home for Steller's jays, which live nearly exclusively in mountain pine forests. One unusual bird here is the gray-crowned rosy-finch that forages in the snow-laden mountains.

Rio Grande Valley

TEXAS

Along with the other southern border states, Texas' Rio Grande Valley is at the center of the annual hummingbird migration and an especially awesome spot to see buff-bellied and ruby-throated hummingbirds flitting about. Persistent birdwatchers might even catch a glimpse or two of a tropical species that may have wandered north of their native habitat.

Tohono Chul Park

TUCSON, ARIZONA

Residing within the Sonoran Desert, this park provides easy walking trails and gardens to view some of the 140 bird species that visit the 49-acre site. A hummingbird garden attracts Costa's and Anna's hummingbirds year-round to sip nectar from salvia, desert willow and other plants. The Wildlife Garden features saguaro cacti where Gila woodpeckers build nests.

The Desert Botanical Garden

PHOENIX, ARIZONA

There's a Desert Wildflower Loop Trail where you can view exhibits on wildflowers while watching hummingbirds. Greater roadrunners nest in candelabra cacti in the Ottosen Entry Garden. Bird lovers will especially enjoy the guided bird walks, which are held nearly every Monday at the 140-acre site.

Grand Teton National Park, Wyoming

Grand Teton National Park

WYOMING

The 300 bird species that have been sighted just south of Yellowstone are as extreme as the landscape here. You can spot both the smallest bird in North America, the Calliope hummingbird, and the largest waterfowl, the trumpeter swan, in this park. With more than 200 miles of trails to explore, you'll never run out of options. Other notable species that have been spotted here include three-toed woodpecker, great gray owl, osprey and Brewer's sparrow.

Yosemite National Park

TOHONO CHUL PARK: RANDY LARSON; YOSEMITE: GOSHIVA/SHUTTERSTOCK;

Sightseeing in Sedona

Visit this scenic destination during its peak hummingbird season.

THE INCREDIBLE rock formations are one thing. The buzz of colorful hummingbird activity is another. Put Sedona on your birder bucket list.

Getting there

No matter where you're coming from, the trip into Red Rock Country is amazing. Fly into Phoenix, grab a car and enjoy a two-hour scenic trip north through small towns and rolling hills along Interstate 17, then a short drive up State Route 179, the Red Rock Scenic Byway.

Highlights

The stars are all here: rufous, broad-tailed, Calliope, black-chinned and Anna's (a year-round resident). The number and variety of the birds in Sedona reach their peak in August. Several hot spots in the area offer up-close, personal views of these birds in large numbers.

Secret spot

For breathtaking views and incredible sunsets, drive the uphill, winding Airport Road to Sedona Airport. An overlook atop a mesa provides a panoramic view of the city below. A quick hike down the hill from the airport leads to one of the city's energy vortexes and more views of classic red rocks.

Spectacular park

Red Rock State Park, with its shaded hummingbird patio and multiple sugar-water feeders, is worth a visit. Hike easy trails on your own, go on a guided nature or bird walk (you might spot a lazuli bunting!) or simply take in the rocky sights of sandstone canyons.

Can't-miss festival

Sedona Hummingbird Festival draws crowds from all over the country. Locals open their backyards and serve breakfast (tickets required) with a side of optimum hummingbird viewing. You can also go on a garden tour, where residents welcome festivalgoers to meander through their gardens and watch hundreds of tiny guests feed. Plus, see banding demonstrations, listen to expert presentations and do guided bird walks. Visit *hummingbirdsociety. org* for registration and ticket information for the festival.

Sedona

ARIZONA

SWORD-BILLED SPLENDOR

Meet the only bird in the world with a bill longer than its body. The 3- to 4-inch bill helps sword-billeds reach the nectar in long, deep flowers that other hummingbirds can't attain. To maintain balance while resting, this bird sits with its bill pointed toward the sky.

A Peek into the Tropics

Ecuador's hummingbirds really stand out. Get to know those with remarkable features—like crowns that look dipped in rainbow dust.

BLACK-TAILED TRAINBEARER

With a small bill and a tail that lives up to its name, this bird is easy to spot. Unlike many of Ecuador's hummingbirds, the black-tailed trainbearer is not a forest dweller but is commonly seen in backyards, most notably in the country's capital city, Quito.

SPARKLING VIOLETEAR

This is a gorgeous bird even before you notice the violet ear tufts that extend past its head. The species is one of the most common in the Andes Mountains, but that doesn't make it any less incredible each time you see it.

Ecuador is the size of Colorado and home to more than 130 hummingbird species.

COLLARED INCA

Somewhat large and exceptionally fast for a hummingbird, the collared inca might not seem, at first glance, to belong in our all-star group. But the contrast of black and white is striking as the bird whizzes by. And if you're lucky enough to see this beauty sit still for a minute, notice the iridescent green feathers intermixed with black ones.

BOOTED RACKET-TAIL

This hummer's forked tail has two extremely long outer feathers, each with a bare streamerlike shaft and brilliant blue, racket-shaped feathers at the tip. The tails flip around in amazing positions, making it one of the most fun hummingbirds to photograph. The color on its "boots" (the puffy feathers at the base of the legs) depends on where you are in the Andes Mountains. On the eastern side, the boots are orange; on the western side, they are bright white.

LONG-TAILED SYLPH

The most distinctive thing about this species is its extremely long tail. The shimmering blue-green color extends up to the crown, making the bird look, in the right light, as if it is glowing. Because this species has a short bill, it sometimes pierces the base of flowers to drink nectar.

More than 1,600 bird species are in Ecuador. That's twice as many as in the U.S.

WIRE-CRESTED THORNTAIL

When you see a male wire-crested thorntail, you immediately notice the incredible wispy green crest, the bold white stripe across the lower back, and his long forked tail. It's difficult to get a good look at this bird because it typically hovers and feeds on flowers high in the tree canopy.

GIANT

There is no better name for the largest hummingbird species in the world. With its slower and deeper wing beats than others, this cinnamon-colored bird may remind you more of a swift or a swallow than a typical hummingbird as it zips by.

Rich in biodiversity, Ecuador is one of only 17 countries classified as megadiverse.

RAINBOW STARFRONTLET

The name itself makes this one of the most special hummingbirds, and the plumage does not disappoint. As if its coppery-colored body and glowing green throat weren't enough, this species sports all the colors of the rainbow on its crown.

The Perfect Shot

We invited some of our favorite photographers to share their incredible shots and their best advice for budding and veteran shutterbugs alike.

TIM FITZHARRIS

Give Yourself Options

Set your camera to its fastest motor drive speed and focus manually. Then shoot hundreds of photos and pick the best ones in postproduction. There's no need for complicated flash setups. For natural results, shoot on overcast days and set your ISO speed at 1000 to 2000, which allows the wings to blur as shown here with this male rufous and female black-chinned.
—Tim Fitzharris

Create Perches

Collect dead branches and twigs, and incorporate them into your gardens and containers. The hummingbirds will use them when they're near their favorite food source, and supply you with an abundance of perched and posed opportunities. I took these three photos of ruby-throats right in my own backyard. **—Bud Hensley**

Look for Photo Ops

When it comes to taking pictures of hummingbirds, I've found the more natural the setting, the better. Like in this photo of an Anna's, which I took in my sister's backyard on the Fourth of July. Her landscaping is designed to attract hummingbirds, and they were really enjoying her Little Redhead crocosmia that day. I try to take advantage of flowers that hummingbirds are attracted to, like bee balm and foxglove. Remember, a great photo opportunity can come from anywhere, so keep your eyes peeled and your camera ready!
—Daniel Ferneding

Know Your Lighting

I'm always looking for a connection between birds and the plants they visit, because it tells the story of pollination, like this male green-crowned brilliant hummingbird posing on an ornamental banana flower (far right). When it's rainy like this, I use fill flash in order to deal with the low light. In general, it's good to have technical knowledge of your camera and flash. This will allow you to capture good photos of these little flying jewels. —Gregory Basco

Get the Right Gear

Hummingbirds are creatures of habit. Train your camera on a bird's preferred perch, prefocus and shoot when it returns. A telephoto lens in the 300 mm to 500 mm range will work perfectly, especially one that can focus as close as 10 feet. Shutter speeds under 1/500th of a second or less will blur the bird's wings, and shutter speeds of 1/2500th will freeze them. Wait for the bird to turn its head, so you can catch the flashy iridescence in the throat patch, like with this Calliope. **—Ed Post**

Keep Exploring

One of my very favorite techniques for photographing hummingbirds is to catch them in flight, while they're coming to feeders or flowers. Setting up an outdoor studio with several flashes can lead to some truly spectacular results. It took several hours of perseverance in challenging lighting conditions to get this shot of a red-tailed comet in the Andes Mountains of central Bolivia, but it was well worth the effort! With more than 300 species of hummingbirds in the world, there is no shortage of incredible species to photograph. **—Glenn Bartley**

A Bucket List for Hummingbird Lovers

These 10 activities, some silly and some seriously cool, are ones every enthusiast should experience.

Davis Mountains State Park in Texas (at right) is known for hosting many species of hummingbirds.

SEVERAL YEARS AGO, I was lucky enough to take a trip to southeastern Arizona where every destination, hike and tour focused on hummingbirds. My fellow travelers and I walked around starry-eyed, clutching cameras and scribbling field notes as we watched the tree branches and feeders. And we weren't disappointed—hummingbirds were everywhere. All told, I spotted 13 different species on that trip, including several rarities.

The experience stuck with me, and made me realize that while watching hummingbirds at backyard sugar-water feeders is pretty wonderful, there are a lot of other ways to indulge your interest in these delightful birds. This list of activities is a good place to start. So what are you waiting for?

Take a hummingbird vacation

Southwestern states including Arizona, California, New Mexico and Texas offer the largest concentration of hummingbirds and a diverse range of hummingbird species. Destinations such as Ramsey Canyon Preserve in Arizona or Davis Mountains State Park in Texas are especially known for plentiful and rare hummingbird sightings. But if such destinations are too far afield for you, take a day trip to a botanical garden that has plenty of sugar-water feeders. You'll see hummingbirds by the dozen, especially during fall migration.

Attend a hummingbird festival

Hummingbird people are good people, and there's no better place to meet those kindred spirits than at a hummingbird festival. You can find these events all over the country. The festivals usually take place in July through September and are concentrated in areas that experience abundant migration activity. The Rockport-Fulton HummerBird Celebration in Texas and the Sedona Hummingbird Festival in Arizona are two of the best.

Start a hummingbird journal

Here's an activity you can do without leaving home. Keep a journal of the hummingbird activity in your yard. Note when the first hummingbird arrives in spring and when the final one departs in fall. How many visit your feeders? How does their activity shift during the day? Notice changing factors such as weather or feeder placement, and write down those funny hummingbird stories, too!

With a little patience, you can learn to feed a hummingbird by hand.

This hummingbird is being measured for banding.

Find a nesting hummingbird

Hummingbirds usually build their intricately engineered nests on tree branches, but sometimes the birds select more visible and unorthodox nesting spots like plant hooks, chandelier-style light fixtures or electrical wires. Any horizontal surface under a protective roof will usually do, though nests can be really hard to find. Gather up your hummingbird-loving friends, and set out on the search.

Get a hummingbird tattoo

Real or temporary, a tattoo is a whimsical—or really devoted—way to acknowledge your love of hummingbirds. Smack that piece of dampened paper to your skin (or visit a reputable tattoo artist), and smile.

Hand-feed a hummingbird

Imagine the thrill of having a tiny hummingbird, which typically weighs 0.1 to 0.2 ounces (less than a marshmallow), alight on your palm. Give hand-feeding a whirl during nesting season or before migration, when the birds are expending a lot of energy and eating a lot of food. Spend time near your feeders, so the birds become accustomed to your presence. Then cover all feeders but one, and hold that remaining feeder in your lap. Not every attempt will be successful, but be patient and keep trying.

Help band hummingbirds

Researchers have been banding birds to gather crucial information about migration, lifespan and population since 1920 as part of the North American Bird Banding Program. Hummingbird banding is an extremely specialized activity—hummingbirds make up less than 1% of birds banded. The banders themselves are an elite group who hold special permits. Participate in the process by volunteering at banding events, which take place at hummingbird festivals, or during migration periods along key flyways.

Recognize hummingbird calls

Experienced birders don't need binoculars to identify birds. They use their ears instead, and usually know a particular bird is nearby well before they spot it. Hummingbirds, though not known for their songs, still make a series of distinct calls. Become attuned to these sounds by finding recordings at websites like *allaboutbirds. org* to learn the calls of different hummingbirds and what they mean.

Share a hummingbird bond

Thinking back to that Arizona hummingbird trip, one of its most enjoyable aspects was the shared experience. That bonding feeling can happen on a trip, at a festival, on your front porch or at places like local schools and senior centers. Look for teaching or volunteering opportunities in your community to pass along what you love about hummingbirds. That's one experience that will surely make your life richer.

DIY hummingbird feeder

Creating your own sugar-water feeder is incredibly simple, and if you're crafty, you've probably already built one or maybe a dozen! For the rest of us, check out sites like Pinterest (or hey, *birdsandblooms.com*) for innumerable ideas. My favorite DIY sugar-water feeders are the ones made from a pretty glass bottle, a stopper and a tube. You can buy the stopper and feeder tube attachments online; just search for "hummingbird feeder tube" to get started.
—*Heather Lamb*

The Truth About Hummingbird Banding

Discover how this highly specialized activity works, what makes it unique, and who are the people behind the research and tracking of these tiny treasures.

Rufous hummingbird among red-flowered currants

TIM FITZHARRIS

1

2

THE BANDING PROCESS

Banding a hummingbird is a very precise and delicate process. It starts with a netting system to capture the bird (1). Then the hummingbird is gently prepared (2) for the tiny band (3). The bander inspects the bird for overall health (4) before letting it go (5).

YOU OFTEN HEAR about the banding of songbirds and raptors—but rarely hummingbirds. It can be done if you understand the intricacies, and approach the task with knowledge and care.

The number of banded hummers is low. Hummingbird banding started long after songbird banding, so researchers don't have nearly as much information on the little fliers as they do on other birds. According to the North American Bird Banding Program operated by the U.S. Geological Survey and the Canadian Wildlife Service, about 309,000 ruby-throated hummingbirds have been banded since 1960. By comparison, more than 30 million songbirds have been banded.

Banding is a useful migration research tool. Most of what we do know about hummingbird migration is because of banding. The data scientists have gathered thus far tell us amazing things. For instance, we know that ruby-throated hummingbirds follow the same migration routes every year.

They also arrive at and leave from stopover points on almost the same date each year, within a few days.

The process does not harm the birds. Hummingbird feeders equipped with curtains, netting or cages are monitored, and when a bird visits, it flips a switch and the netting comes down or the cage closes. This is a more effective method for capturing hummingbirds than the large mist nets usually used in songbird banding.

Hummingbird bands are incredibly tiny. As you might expect, the bands that go around the leg of a hummingbird are minuscule—so small they fit around a toothpick or safety pin. Typically, they measure just 1.27-1.52 mm in diameter and 1.6 mm wide. Each band bears a letter prefix followed by a four-digit number. The letter represents a five-digit number that is too big to print on the diminutive band.

You can help. If you think you have a rare hummingbird visiting your backyard or a hummer that seems to be staying for the winter,

banders may be interested in your guest. Increasingly, western hummingbirds are showing up in the East, and you can help researchers find out why by alerting banders. Check out *hummingbirdsplus.org* to see a list of eastern banders.

Hummingbird banders are an elite group. Only about 150 people in the U.S. hold permits to band hummingbirds. They're authorized to take part in the program after completing rigorous training. Unlike other bird bands, those made for hummers are cut and sized by the banders themselves. Banders are also expected to follow a code of ethics.

Banding is quick. Hummingbirds aren't in the banders' hands for long. Banders work swiftly to record species, sex, age, weight, measurements and the birds' overall condition. After that, banders sometimes offer the birds a quick drink at a sugar-water feeder before promptly releasing them.

Timing and location are important. It makes sense to kick up hummingbird banding efforts during migration. Banders gather at crucial flyway areas. Alabama's Fort Morgan Banding Station, for instance, is the first landfall and the last departure location along the Gulf of Mexico for thousands of migratory birds, including ruby-throats. Banding in southeast Arizona is especially important, because this part of the international flyway hosts the greatest diversity of hummingbird species anywhere north of Mexico. Researchers based in Arizona are able to examine tropical species heading north as well as common migrants like the rufous and Calliope hummingbirds.

Banders are banders for life. Take Bob and Martha Sargent, who founded the nonprofit Hummer/Bird Study Group to track migrating hummingbirds and songbirds. Since they started their original banding station in their Clay, Alabama, backyard, more than 30,000 ruby-throateds have been banded there. Other devoted banders spend years researching hummingbirds, running websites to spread awareness and doing banding demonstrations. So it's true: Once a hummingbird bander, always a hummingbird bander.

WATCH A BANDING DEMONSTRATION
See hummingbird banding for yourself at one of these locations.

BISBEE, ARIZONA
Fifteen hummingbird species nest in or migrate through the vicinity of the Southeastern Arizona Bird Observatory. The observatory hosts banding demonstrations from spring through early fall, open to the public. For dates and times, check out *sabo.org*.

LEASBURG, MISSOURI
Watch researchers band ruby-throated hummingbirds and learn about the birds' lives. The banding takes place at Onondaga Cave State Park on various days throughout summer. See *mostateparks.com* for details.

CHAPTER 6
Hummingbird Tales

Across the nation, *Birds & Blooms* readers share interesting stories and stunning photographs of hummingbirds at their beautiful, beguiling and curious best.

Every spring and throughout most of the year, 50 to 100 hummingbirds, like this male Calliope, visit my 11 feeders. They drink about 2 gallons of sugar water per day! April is my favorite month because I've had as many as six species show up then—Anna's, rufous, Calliope, black-chinned, Allen's and a single Costa's.

Elijah Gildea REDDING, CALIFORNIA

A female ruby-throated hummingbird sampled the Black and Blue salvia near my pool. Hummingbirds are so joyful to watch as they dance among the abundant summer blooms. They are especially fond of salvia, and constantly on the lookout for competitors for the nectar.

Liz Tabb
ELIZABETHTOWN, KENTUCKY

It was near the end of the season, and this feisty ruby-throated hummingbird was buzzing around, fighting over feeders and filling up on nectar. I always miss these charismatic little birds once they leave because they fill my summer months with happiness.

Cynthia Evert-Mattsson
MORRISVILLE, NORTH CAROLINA

This beautiful Anna's hummingbird

appeared as I was taking photos near the Bay Bridge in San Francisco. I love this image because there's such great detail in both the bird and the salvia flowers.

Rachel VanDemark
LONGWOOD, FLORIDA

I always look forward to the

first hummingbird of the season. The year we put out our hummingbird feeders during the first weekend in April, which is a little early for us, lo and behold, this broad-tailed hummingbird showed up early! I was delighted to see the other hummingbirds follow suit just a week later.

Kristen Clark
TIJERAS, NEW MEXICO

A ruby-throated hummingbird at a glowing hibiscus bloom shows you just how small this bird is! This was my first attempt at growing hibiscus, but it is pretty hardy and should come back year after year, even here in Indiana.

Carol Holliday TERRE HAUTE, INDIANA

While visiting a local park in Phoenix, Arizona, I noticed this male Costa's feeding among the hummingbird bush flowers. It was a bright, sunny day, which allowed me to use a fast shutter speed to freeze the hummingbird in flight.

Hayley Crews PLACERVILLE, CALIFORNIA

An Anna's
hummingbird
spends winters in
my yard. One day, I sat
at the window waiting
for the bird to light on
a snowy butterfly bush.
Eventually, the beautiful
winter jewel obliged.

Kristi Gruel
SNOHOMISH,
WASHINGTON

During a
Fourth of July
parade, a co-worker
noticed a hummingbird
in its nest on a very low
branch. With so many
people sitting under
it and walking nearby,
we were amazed it did
not fly off. We checked
that nest every few
days until the babies
left. I like to call this
shot "Full House."

Deb DeCosta
HARWICH,
MASSACHUSETTS

On my way to work, I walk past a restaurant. One day, I noticed a group of Anna's hummingbirds buzzing around, and I captured several photos, including one of this bright male posing among the eatery's Christmas lights.

Rick Kleinosky
CORVALLIS, OREGON

This leucistic Anna's is one of the most beautiful hummingbirds I have ever photographed. It was feeding on giant buffet-size flowers at the University of California's Santa Cruz Arboretum & Botanic Garden. The handsome bird is without pigmentation in its feathers, giving it the cool snowy look.

Elijah Gildea
REDDING, CALIFORNIA

From my dining room window, I noticed this ruby-throated hummingbird perched on a canna leaf near my oscillating sprinkler. Each time the spray came around, the bird flapped its wings and stretched toward the water. When the shower rotated away, the ruby-throated sat patiently, waiting. I'm glad I was inside, because I was able to watch for several minutes unnoticed. I garden for these special moments!

Beverly Thevenin CHESTERTON, INDIANA

What a little backyard bully! This male ruby-throated was practically strutting to show his dominance, protecting his territory from atop a dahlia bud near the back deck. My coming and going didn't bother him until I got out my camera, and that's when he darted away. I set the camera on a tripod with a remote and hid inside to get this photo.

Purnell Hopson SEAFORD, VIRGINIA

This male ruby-throated hummingbird

landed on a branch with the American flag in the background. It's the perfect photo for the Fourth of July!

Joey Herron
FAIRMONT,
WEST VIRGINIA

Rufous hummingbirds were chasing

one another near my driveway, so I hid in the corner and kept snapping photos. I like this one for the way that his little feet are in landing position but are not yet touching the twig.

Renae Tolbert
REDDING, CALIFORNIA

The hummingbirds were zipping around the sugar-water feeders, so I patiently sat on my front porch with my camera at the ready. I took a lot of pictures before finally getting this one. This particular male ruby-throated was very protective of "his" feeder and was trying to scare off all the others.

Elisabeth Kelley
MILLBROOK, ALABAMA

I snapped this photo of an Anna's hummingbird one year on Valentine's Day. It was enjoying the much-needed rain after some hot, dry Arizona weather. I like how its torso is shaped like a heart in this image.

Lisa Swanson
MARICOPA, ARIZONA

This black-chinned hummingbird family of three settled
into a tree near our house. The nest was the size of a small espresso cup and the
eggs looked like white jelly beans. I felt so fortunate to be able to photograph the
babies as they matured and fledged.

Melissa Cheatwood BERTRAM, TEXAS

One rainy afternoon in June, a female ruby-throated took a little break from buzzing around the flowers and feeders to perch on the hummingbird swing. She stayed there for some time, and it was fun to grab the camera and capture the moment. I love how fluffed and ruffled her feathers are from the rain.

Lauren Slack WATERVILLE, MAINE

This young male Anna's perfectly exudes the stunning beauty of all hummingbirds. He is busy, yet peaceful, as he sips nectar from purple sage.

Paula Fleitell
EUGENE, OREGON

Here in Las Vegas, we have the pleasure of seeing and hosting hummingbirds all year long. This beautiful male Costa's frequently visits my backyard, and I was lucky enough to snap his photo.

Mark Rasmussen
LAS VEGAS, NEVADA

This male rufous enjoyed a light shower in Astoria, Oregon. I love his bold attitude and bright colors.

Trish Nevan
TERREBONNE, OREGON

Living in North Carolina, I see only ruby-throated hummingbirds. While on a trip to southern Arizona, I was thrilled to capture this photo of a male broad-billed hummingbird.

Linda Jahn
HICKORY, NORTH CAROLINA

I waited out a late afternoon storm in hopes of having the opportunity to explore. After the downpour subsided, I captured this broad-billed hummingbird finding the perfect perch on a beautiful agave plant. How lucky!

Joanna Proffitt SURPRISE, ARIZONA

Hummingbirds are creatures of habit and they make their
rounds from flower to flower. Once I've figured out their pattern, I begin timing
and listening for them, which allows me to get prepared and set for each round.
Typically, I start photographing them when they reach 15-minute routine intervals.
I use my Canon with a 400mm prime lens at a 10-foot focal length.

Mike Bond SUMTER, SOUTH CAROLINA

A lot of people start their day with a cup of coffee. Not me! I begin each day outside watching hummingbirds. There's nothing like the cool morning air and the sound of whirring wings among the stillness and quiet of my rural yard. This particular morning I was lucky enough to capture this sweet ruby-throated guarding her flower from other hummers.

Julie Kirk
OBION, TENNESSEE

My mother loved hummingbirds, so I learned how to photograph them for her. After watching them, I have come to enjoy their antics, too! I noticed this female ruby-throated hummingbird darting among my flowers, and I quickly grabbed my camera and followed her around the yard. She was nose deep in the daylily, and I was waiting for her to come out. To my surprise she turned around and took a seat in the daylily! I was lucky enough to get a few shots of her before she took off again.

Vickie Tuskan
EVELETH, MINNESOTA

I gave two grandsons

cameras for Christmas. During a visit earlier this year, my husband and I took them on a bird walk through San Elijo Lagoon in Cardiff, California. Our cameras clicked away when we saw ducks and egrets, and the excitement was especially high for our fledgling photographers, ages 7 and 4. Imagine the joy when this beautiful male Costa's perched in front of us. His brilliant plumage caught the light perfectly.

Marilyn Barnes
COBLESKILL, NEW YORK

A few years ago, some new, feathered neighbors moved into my orange tree. It wasn't until the female hummingbird finished her nest that I spotted her. I put up a feeder and started taking photos when she seemed to tolerate my presence, photographing her babies until they were strong enough to leave the nest. The mother was an amazing caregiver, and it was incredible to watch these tiny birds grow.

Pete Ritz SCOTTSDALE, ARIZONA

When we moved to Orlando, Florida, we had a new home but no garden. I love taking photos of hummingbirds, and back in Texas I attracted them to my backyard flower gardens to enjoy their beauty. I worked hard to design and plant three new hummingbird gardens. After months of tough yardwork, it all paid off when my landscape became a magnet for hummingbirds, like this ruby-throated.

Gilberto Sanchez ORLANDO, FLORIDA

I watched this hummingbird fly from flower to flower, drinking nectar. It left for a short time, then came back for another drink. Hoping to get a picture, I grabbed my camera and a chair and sat near the blooms. I was lucky to get several shots, but this one made me smile. The delicate gladiolus petals draped the bird like a tiny protective cover.

Shirley Hancock SINKS GROVE, WEST VIRGINIA

I've sometimes seen an Anna's hummingbird after the first snow, but it would leave after filling up on nectar or after my feeder froze. Then I tried a new approach: two feeders. When we had freezing weather and then snow, I defrosted one while the other was out, so that my Anna's always had food. This male quickly figured out my routine and seemed to pose for me while I replaced his favorite feeder.

Lynnette Mammino
GRASS VALLEY,
CALIFORNIA

This sweet Anna's hummingbird found a home in our garden one winter. I wanted to take a picture, then had the idea of putting an ornament on the branch where our feathered friend liked to perch. When snow started falling, I waited patiently, and soon she came and sat in just the right place. What a marvelous way to say merry Christmas!

Natalia Karapunarly
SALEM, OREGON

While hiking in Rocky Mountain National Park in Colorado, I could hear hummingbirds. I waited for a while and saw this broad-tailed hummingbird coming to the same perch over and over. I quickly extended my tripod to get eye level with the bird and started shooting. I was so lucky to get this photo right as the hummer was applying its brakes to land!

Sharon Draker
BANDERA, TEXAS

While I was trying to capture an action shot of this hummingbird, it sat on the stem of a flower. I quietly said, "Please sit still," and to my surprise, it looked right at me and lit up, doing exactly as I asked it to. After a few clicks, the hummingbird was gone.

Joyce Rickert
SALEM, OREGON

My wife has fed visiting ruby-throated hummingbirds for years. We live on the Tombigbee River and every September we see a dramatic increase in hummingbird numbers. We go through so much sugar, I've started calling them "humming pigs." We like to sit a few feet away from the feeders, and they buzz around us like a swarm of bees. Although they're nearly impossible to count, there's no doubt we've had at least a hundred birds on our porch at one time. We enjoy it while it lasts, but by the middle of October, they're gone.

Larry Knight ALICEVILLE, ALABAMA

I feed, photograph and study about 15 hummingbirds that regularly visit my three feeders. I also plant for their appetites: orange trumpet vine, rose of Sharon, pink honeysuckle and coneflower. On this particular day, the Nevada wind was really whipping the flowers around when this hummingbird landed and had to hold on with both feet! He bobbed up and down for a good minute before he was able to move up and get his nectar.

Kathy Port GARDNERVILLE, NEVADA

When this female rufous

wasn't visiting the feeder on our deck, she perched prettily on a cactus flower. But when I was ready with my camera, would she sit on the cactus? No! I sat for about nine hours over several days trying to get such a shot. While I kept still, she would hover a few inches away. I could feel the air from her beating wings fanning my face. It was a beautiful experience. Finally she rewarded my patience! And of all my hummingbird photos since, this one remains my favorite.

Carol Mattson
PARADISE, CALIFORNIA

This young female Costa's

is one of two chicks her mother raised in my lighthouse wind chime. She frequently visits and is very protective of her feeder. On this day, she perched nicely for my camera in the ocotillo bush.

Luisa Daniel
LA QUINTA, CALIFORNIA

Every year I plant zinnias in my flower garden, and when they bloom I can sometimes get photos of the hummingbirds enjoying them. This female ruby-throated's posture gives her such a fun expression, with her head upturned and her claws balancing on the flower's edge.

Tammi Frick
ALTO, MICHIGAN

To capture photos of these black-chinned and Anna's hummingbirds around a bottlebrush plant, I had to get clever. I began by photographing them at the feeder with my high-speed setup. Then, to get the bottlebrush into the picture, I sprayed the plant with sugar water and switched it with the feeder.

Don Jedlovec
FREMONT, CALIFORNIA

Growing up in the city, I never really saw a hummingbird up close. Once I moved to the suburbs, I started planting flowers in my backyard. The hummingbirds absolutely love the bee balm, and it's exciting to see them come back every year. Now I'm adding even more plants to attract as many hummingbirds as I can!

Carmen Rugel MIDDLETOWN, RHODE ISLAND

The sun was peeking over the tree line, and I stood with a cup of coffee watching God's creation unfold. The bloom on the orchid cactus my sister gave me was opening, and I wanted a picture of it to send to her. Right then, a hummingbird flitted over to check out the flower. With the sun shining perfectly on the bloom, I captured this wonderful moment.

Patrick Henderson MATTHEWS, NORTH CAROLINA

Gladiolas are one of my all-time favorite summer blooms, and while I was taking photos of the ones in my garden, I noticed I had company. A juvenile ruby-throated hummingbird was also interested in the blooms! I shouldn't have been too surprised because hummingbirds like the color red, but it really brought a smile to my face.

Patty Jennings
STACYVILLE, MAINE

This male ruby-throated hummingbird was extremely friendly one summer. We took this photo in our flower garden late in the evening, which is when this guy would sit a lot. Luckily, we were able to get pretty close to him for the photo. After he left, a younger, much more aggressive, male hummer came along. We sure enjoyed our up-close interactions with this friendly fellow while they lasted.

Dennis McNeill
CLIO, MICHIGAN

This male Costa's hummingbird is actually guarding "his" feeder. Any time another Costa's, black-chinned or Anna's would land on the feeder, he would dash out from his hiding place in this pomegranate bush, scare away the competition and return to the exact same branch. His stubbornness made it easy for me to set up my camera, aim and get several good pictures.

Carla Ritter
IVINS, UTAH

This male Calliope was the first arrival of the year, stopping by our yard in mid-April. During the colder spring weather, he would perch on this stick close to the feeder. The blurry pink background is thanks to our crabapple tree, which was in full bloom across the yard.

Bill Bolster
MEDICAL LAKE,
WASHINGTON

There was a lot of congestion at the feeders one summer evening, but this female ruby-throated hummingbird waited on a black-eyed Susan until all the drama at the "water cooler" was over before taking her turn. I've seen hummingbirds in trees and on feeder perches and posts, but this was the first time I'd witnessed one using a black-eyed Susan as a resting place.

Jon Montgomery DU QUOIN, ILLINOIS

A leucistic Anna's hummingbird visited the Australian Garden at the UCSC Arboretum, a public garden about 60 miles from my home. I love hummingbirds, so I had to drive there to see this rare bird for myself. I'd heard that seeing it was hit or miss, but I got extremely lucky. The bird streaked across the sky like a white bullet, then hovered over the blossoms in front of me. As my heart raced, I took as many photos as I could until it sped off as fast as it had flown in! I've been back to look for it many times since that day. Sometimes I've seen it and sometimes I haven't, but each time I do, I'm still in awe at the sight—and grateful that it graced me with its presence.

Sally Rae Kimmel LAFAYETTE, CALIFORNIA

Hummingbirds are difficult to photograph because they move so quickly. But I managed to get this rufous looking right at me while I captured the rapid movement of its tiny wings.

Maralee Park
BEND, OREGON

The only time we normally see rufous hummingbirds in our part of Louisiana is when they winter here, which is what this little guy did in our yard. It was so fun and exciting watching him. He had a feeder all to himself, yet he was very protective of it, running off mockingbirds and cardinals alike. When his juvenile coloration started to change, I knew he wouldn't be staying much longer. Sure enough, two days after the last of his bright adult feathers came in, he left for more northerly parts. I was lucky to have a couple of days to photograph him, and even more so to get this amazing shot!

Helena Reynolds
VENTRESS, LOUISIANA

Hummingbirds in my backyard

often sit on sunflower leaves, although the leaves look more like branches next to them! This squirt is just a youngster, but a feisty one. It sits on this leaf or one nearby and guards the feeder for itself, successfully chasing the older birds away. Of course, every now and then, even a tiny hummingbird like this one must take time from guard duty to scratch an itch!

Sherri Woodbridge
MEDFORD, OREGON

I'm an avid hobby photographer, and some

of my favorite subjects are the hummingbirds in my yard. When it was hot and dry for quite a while here in northwest Washington, I propped up the hose so it offered a gentle shower for the hummingbirds to play in. They took to it within minutes, and I was fortunate enough to get some photos and a video. I hooked up their shower several times, and they always took advantage of it.

Cathy Scott BOW, WASHINGTON

One rainy Saturday morning, my husband and I noticed a ruby-throated hummingbird relishing the rain. These birds are usually in motion, so it was a peaceful sight to see this hummingbird perched contentedly, neck stretched with its head to the sky, truly enjoying the moment. I snapped this photo through our kitchen window. I love the idea that this little bird was stopping to enjoy the cool rain!

Mary Meyer EYOTA, MINNESOTA

After reading that the iochroma, or mini angel's trumpet, is a hummingbird magnet, I knew I had to find one. The local nurseries weren't familiar with the plant, but I was able to find and buy one online by searching for "Iochroma Royal Queen." This photo proves that hummingbirds really do like the plant! The flowers are beautiful, and I'm happy I was able to add this cultivar to my yard.

Barbara Richardson MARION, SOUTH CAROLINA

This female rufous guarded the feeder in my yard, attacking other hummingbirds, then returning to this perch as lookout. What makes this photo special is her protruding tongue, which shows a flash of the beautiful bird's movements.

Allen Livingston
HUNTINGTON, UTAH

After visiting Coyote Hills Regional Park in Fremont, California, and seeing how much its resident Anna's and Allen's hummingbirds enjoyed their nectar garden fountain, I decided to put one in my own backyard. I put this fountain together myself using a large ceramic bowl, a metal stand and a bamboo fountain kit. It was an instant hit with the two young Anna's that hatched in one of our privet trees that February.

Melanie Hofmann
BERKELEY, CALIFORNIA

This lovely male Anna's hummingbird was perched in a pomegranate tree in my neighbor's backyard. He was fiercely guarding the feeder that hung nearby. When any other birds approached, he chased them away, then flew back to his perch. Hummingbirds are so small, yet so aggressive when protecting their territory. I admired this little guy's persistence in guarding his spot. The look in his eye shows a lot of strength for such a small bird. He has the eye of the tiger!

Robin Hardin
LOS ALAMOS, CALIFORNIA

Southen California is often drought-stricken, and water-wise plants like this aloe plant are encouraged. Luckily, hummingbirds are frequent visitors to the aloe blooms in my yard. The perfect combination of wildlife and drought tolerant plants makes an amazing photo op!

Koji Kanemoto
LONG BEACH, CALIFORNIA

I took this photo in a friend's yard. I love hummingbirds and have some in my garden, but my friend has many more than I do. The male ruby-throated was the only one of his species I saw that day in May—the rest were black-chinned. I took several hundred photos, and when I got home I was thrilled to see that I had captured this fabulous shot.

Johnny Bliznak ABILENE, TEXAS

CHAPTER 7

Ask the Experts

Birds & Blooms birding and gardening pros Kenn and Kimberly Kaufman, and Melinda Myers answer both common and perplexing hummingbird questions.

Q Is it necessary to boil the sugar-water mixture for use in hummingbird feeders? I just stir until the sugar is dissolved.

Amy Kernes BREA, CALIFORNIA

Kenn and Kimberly: Opinions differ on the importance of boiling the mixture. We always do it to neutralize some impurities that might be in the water or sugar. Besides, sugar dissolves more easily in hot water. But as soon as the feeder is outdoors, contaminants will get into the water anyway, brought by hummingbirds, insects or just a breeze. So at best, boiling the mixture keeps it fresh a little longer. If your water is good and your time is limited, washing the feeder thoroughly and often is more important than boiling the sugar-water mixture.

Q I've heard that when sugar water freezes and then thaws, the sugar settles to the bottom of the feeder. Is this true? Does it cause a problem for the birds?

John Taylor GRANTS PASS, OREGON

Kenn and Kimberly: Opinions vary on whether it's OK to freeze surplus sugar water, so we advise erring on the side of caution. We've been feeding hummingbirds for decades, and we've never frozen our spare food. However, we do refrigerate it for up to a week.

If you have feeders up in weather so cold that the sugar water freezes, we suggest thawing and cleaning out the feeders, then adding a fresh batch—just to be sure you're keeping those flying jewels safe and healthy. You can also bring your feeders indoors at night to prevent freezing, but it's important to put them back out first thing in the morning.

Ruby-throated hummingbird

Q We're selling our house, and I'm concerned the new owners will not keep the hummingbird feeders filled. What will happen?

Vincent Staley
FREDERICKSBURG, VIRGINIA

Kenn and Kimberly: We appreciate your concern, but hummingbirds are adaptable and good at finding new places to live. In natural habitats. Consider the fact that concentrations of flowers may change over time. Hummingbirds have to be able to move around and find new food sources. Of course, if you can talk to the new residents of your home, you could try to inspire them with stories about the magic of hummingbirds and tell them the rewards of keeping the feeders filled and clean.

Q Help! I switched hummingbird feeders and now the population in my backyard has decreased. The ratio for sugar water is the same. What is the problem?

Judy Mahlau
CHARLOTTE, NORTH CAROLINA

Kenn and Kimberly: Hummingbirds can be rather persnickety about a change in feeders, so a bit of patience might be in order here. Also consider that, depending on the timing, it might be a coincidence. We've found that when the flowers in our garden are in full bloom, traffic to our hummingbird feeders diminishes noticeably. The hummingbirds are still around, but they visit the feeders less when they have more menu options.

Ruby-throated
hummingbird

Q. Two years ago, I had up to 10 hummingbirds in my yard at a time. Last year, spring arrived early so I placed my feeders out in March, but there was no sign of hummingbirds. What could be happening?

Ida Schroeder ARDMORE, OKLAHOMA

Kenn and Kimberly: It's hard to say without knowing more details about your locale, but several factors could be at play. In a warm spring when flowers start blooming early, people may actually see fewer hummingbirds at their feeders and garden plants, because so much natural food is available elsewhere.

Q. My mother-in-law has hummingbirds from spring to fall. I live only 15 minutes south of her and I only see hummingbirds in the fall, as they start to head toward Mexico. Can just a few miles make a difference as to where these birds decide to live?

Michelle Hesse
LAKE CHARLES, LOUISIANA

Kenn and Kimberly: It could have something to do with the habitat in your neighborhood. In migration, hummingbirds may show up anywhere, but in nesting season they are more selective about their surroundings. They look for a special mix of trees, flowers and open areas. You can "sweeten the deal" in your yard by planting nectar-producing flowers. We've also found that hummingbirds can be somewhat picky about feeders. We've used many different kinds of hummingbird feeders, from the conventional style with a glass bottle and plastic bottom to whimsical feeders shaped like strawberries, most with good results. But there have been a few designs that the hummingbirds refused to use. So if everything else about your yard seems right for summer hummers, you might try experimenting with different types of feeders from the ones you've been using.

ALL GROWN UP
By summer's end, juvenile ruby-throateds are about the same size as adults. Males only have a few red throat feathers, not the bright, mature gorget you see on adults.

Q. Were these two juvenile ruby-throated hummingbirds flirting or fighting?

Joseph Brown CHRISTIANSBURG, VIRGINIA

Kenn and Kimberly: That's a great action shot! Hummingbirds seem to put a lot of their abundant energy into chasing each other. Sometimes there are practical reasons for their aggression, such as when they're defending a favorite patch of blooms to protect their nectar supply, but other times they seem to be acting out on their generally spunky nature. Young hummingbirds don't mate until the year after they hatch, so these juveniles were probably just horsing around, not flirting.

Q I took this photo near Scottsdale, Arizona. I think it's an immature male, but is it a black-chinned or an Anna's?

Steve Dummermuth Jr.

CEDAR RAPIDS, IOWA

Kenn and Kimberly: Young male hummingbirds are tricky to identify, because they're often somewhere between the appearance of a female and an adult male. We think this is a young male Costa's hummingbird for several reasons. The dark outline of the throat patch, extending down and back below the eye, is very typical of Costa's at this stage, and so is the patch of pinkish purple on the lower throat. Also, the breast and sides are clear whitish—most Anna's and black-chinneds show more of a gray-green wash on the sides.

Q There was a ruby-throated hummingbird and titmouse that looked like they were playing tag in my backyard. What were they doing?

Tom Balkwill LITHIA, FLORIDA

Kenn and Kimberly: We sometimes see hummingbirds that appear to be chasing small songbirds, like goldfinches or warblers. It's fascinating, and we don't completely know why it happens. Hummingbirds sometimes aggressively defend their favorite flowers or feeders from other hummers, but a songbird wouldn't be competing for those food sources, so there's no reason to chase them. The best explanation is that birds have individual personalities, and some hummingbirds are just extra feisty, chasing other birds to burn off energy.

Q How rare is an albino hummingbird?

Maurita Denney CAMP VERDE, ARIZONA

Kenn and Kimberly: A white hummingbird flitting around flowers is one of the most amazing sights in nature. True albinos are extremely rare, with only a few ever documented in the wild; they're recognized by pure white feathers and pink eyes, bill and feet. Also rare but slightly more common are leucistic hummingbirds, which look all white or mostly white but have normal-colored eyes, bills and feet. Lack of pigment makes birds more vulnerable to predators, and they may not live as long as birds with normal colors. One or two white hummingbirds are reported somewhere practically every year, but the chances of seeing one in your own yard are probably less than one in a million.

Leucistic black-chinned hummingbird

HOW ALBINISM HAPPENS
For a bird to be albino, both of its parents have to carry the uncommon recessive genes that produce rare white offspring.

Ruby-throated
hummingbird

Q. I have heard that you should make sugar water strong for hummingbirds when they first arrive in spring. Is this true?

Evelyn Goodspeed WITHERBEE, NEW YORK

Kenn and Kimberly: When the hummers first arrive in spring, it's not necessary to sweeten up your mixture. We always recommend mixing 1 cup white granulated sugar with 4 cups water. Boil it to help reduce any impurities in the solution and then let it cool. You should steer clear of brown sugar, powdered sugar, honey, red dye or any other ingredient but plain white sugar.

Q I saw a hummingbird hanging upside down from my feeder by one foot. As I neared, it flew away. What happened to it?

Margaret Hocker
METROPOLIS, ILLINOIS

Kenn and Kimberly: Hummingbirds have a bizarre way of conserving energy. Usually at night, during periods of cold and sometimes when they're perched at a feeder, hummingbirds can enter a deep, sleeplike state known as torpor, when all body functions slow dramatically. Their metabolism slows by as much as 95 percent, and heart rate and body temperature drop significantly. Torpor allows them to conserve precious energy and survive some surprisingly low temperatures. Hummingbirds are tough birds!

Q For two weeks last winter, a rufous hummingbird visited. Is this unusual for north-central Florida in January? We usually have ruby-throateds.

Walton Robey OCALA, FLORIDA

Kenn and Kimberly: Years ago, we would have said it was very unusual. At one time, almost all rufous hummingbirds spent the winter in southern Mexico. But these little pioneers have been expanding their winter range into the southeastern U.S. for the last few decades, and hundreds now stay through the season along the Gulf Coast from Texas to Florida, and north as far as the Carolinas. The ruby-throated is still the expected hummingbird in Florida for most of the year, but midwinter, you're just as likely to spot a rufous.

Rufous hummingbird at Rocky Mountain bee plant

LEFT: ISTOCK.COM/CELTICSKY; FAR RIGHT: STEVE AND DAVE MASLOWSKI

Q Ants get into the sugar water in my feeders, keeping the hummingbirds away. What can I do?

Margaret Gill SLAUGHTER, LOUISIANA

Kenn and Kimberly: Ants cause big problems at hummingbird feeders. One solution is to attach an ant moat above the feeder. This is a cup that wraps around the hanger and is filled with plain water, which ants can't cross. It keeps them from continuing down to the feeder itself. Some feeders even come with an ant moat attached or built in. It takes extra effort to keep the moat filled, but it allows you to keep attracting hummingbirds. We strongly advise against trying to stop ants by wrapping sticky material around the pole—there's a high risk that birds will get caught in it.

Q I see hummingbirds flying to the blue spruce in my yard. What are they after?

Loretta McClincy BELLEFONTE, PENNSYLVANIA

Birds & Blooms editors: Besides nectar, hummingbirds also eat—and feed their babies—small insects, which they gather from flowers, shrubs and trees. In the case of the blue spruce, the sap the tree produces is also a nourishing food for them. Often, yellow-bellied sapsuckers will drill holes in spruce trunks to release pools of sweet sap.

Female ruby-throated hummingbirds feed insects to their young because they are a good source of protein.

Q We get Anna's hummingbirds here, but we've never seen this bird (above) before. It showed up for a week in April and sat on the feeder for hours at a time, even at night in the dark. What kind is this?

Pam Brown KENMORE, WASHINGTON

Kenn and Kimberly: Identifying a female hummingbird from a single photo can be very challenging, but we think this is probably just an odd Anna's hummingbird. Color pattern and wing structure rule out every species except Anna's and Costa's hummingbirds, and Costa's is a bird of the Desert Southwest that would be a very rare visitor in Washington. Unfortunately, this bird may have been ill, which would explain why it looked unfamiliar to you and why it would just sit on the feeder for long periods.

Costa's, like this male, weigh in at only one-tenth of an ounce. Their crouched posture makes them look even smaller.

Q. Two kinds of hummingbirds visit our yard: black-chinneds and Costa's. One is a young male Costa's whose throat patch is just beginning to show, and I always wonder how old he is. What is the life span of a hummingbird?

Terry Burkhart LANDERS, CALIFORNIA

Kenn and Kimberly: These tiny creatures don't live long. Based on banding studies, 7 or 8 years is a ripe old age for most hummingbirds in the wild. Ruby-throated hummingbirds have lived 9 years, and one banded female broad-tailed hummingbird in Colorado made it to 12. A zoo that's properly set up to care for these birds may stretch longevity: Two black-chinned hummingbirds at the Arizona-Sonora Desert Museum in Tucson lived to 13 or 14 years old. We don't have much information on the Costa's hummingbird, but a male with his gorget (throat patch) just developing would be a little less than 1 year old.

Q The hummingbirds love the flowers on this mystery plant, but my husband and I are stumped. Can you identify it?

Darlene Cameron
CASA GRANDE, ARIZONA

Melinda: This hummingbird favorite is tree tobacco (*Nicotiana glauca*). It's native to South America, but can be found growing in sandy and gravelly locations and near old dwellings in much of the Southwest. Hardy in zones 10 and 11 and grown as an annual elsewhere, it grows 6 to 10 feet tall. Tree tobacco flowers much of the summer (where hardy) and late in the season when grown as an annual. It thrives in full sun to partial shade and moist, well-draining soil. Let me give you a warning about this plant, though. This plant is considered invasive and a risk to displace native plants in the Southwest. While it's pretty, make sure you don't encourage it, give it to friends or spread it around.

Q Orioles visit my hummingbird feeders and make a real mess. How can I get them to use the oriole feeder instead?

Bonnie Ramsburg GRANTSVILLE, MARYLAND

Kenn and Kimberly: We've yet to find an oriole feeder that orioles prefer to hummingbird feeders. We didn't want to give up feeding both kinds of birds, so we found another approach. To avoid having all of our precious sugar water dumped on the ground by marauding orioles, we simply bought the type of hummingbird feeder that comes with a large glass bottle for the sugar water. This glass reservoir will hold nearly 4 cups of nectar, and the heft of it—no matter how much you fill it—is enough to keep the feeder hanging evenly under the weight of even the hungriest oriole!

This baby praying mantis is as green as the leaf it is perched on. It blends right in with its surroundings as it sits motionless and waits for prey.

Q I've removed a praying mantis from my hummingbird feeder several times and even trimmed the plants away from the feeder, but the insect keeps coming back. What can I do to keep it away?

Terry Hathcock
MILLINGTON, TENNESSEE

Kenn and Kimberly: A large mantis is fully capable of catching and eating hummingbirds, so this is a serious issue. Once an individual mantis develops a fixation on your feeder, it may come back repeatedly to try to nab a hummingbird. You could catch the mantis and take it away—for example, drive to some natural habitat a few miles away and release it there. If that seems like too much effort and you don't want to use lethal methods, it's best to take the feeder down for a few days and let the mantis find a different hunting spot.

Q. For several days, we noticed that about eight Anna's hummingbirds swarmed around one feeder at the same time each evening. What can you tell us about this behavior?

William Herrmannsfeldt
LOS ALTOS, CALIFORNIA

Birds & Blooms editors: Waning daylight is probably why so many hummingbirds flock to a feeder at the same time each evening. They tend to feed more just before dark so they have enough energy to survive the night. With the sun setting at about the same time each night, the birds stock up at that time, too.

Q. The area around my patio is wet and muddy after it rains. How can I get the soil to dry, and what flowers friendly for hummingbirds and butterflies grow best in these conditions?

Donna Maples MIDDLETON, WISCONSIN

Melinda: First, improve the drainage by adding several inches of organic matter to the top 12 inches of soil. Then plant perennial flowers that tolerate moist to wet soils. For early spring blooms, grow camassia, daffodils and leopard's bane. They all provide a welcome splash of color and offer nectar to early season pollinators. Don't be alarmed if the leopard's bane goes dormant in the summer.

For summer blooms, add vertical interest and hummingbird appeal with Siberian iris. And consider white-flowered smooth penstemon and blue marsh phlox for midseason color. Cardinal flower brings a vibrant splash of red and attracts hummingbirds, and tall purple prairie blazing star, giant blue lobelia, turtlehead and Joe Pye weed continue the color into fall. Finish the growing season with moisture tolerant native crested aster. Include sedges for added texture and to help unify the planting.

Female
ruby-throated
hummingbird

Q I've had these flowers in my garden for a couple of years now, but I've never seen a hummingbird at them before. What lures hummingbirds to sunflowers?

John Yinger COLUMBUS, OHIO

Kenn and Kimberly: Sunflowers look very different from the red tubular flowers famous for attracting hummingbirds. Sunflowers, daisies and related plants have composite flowers—that is, each "bloom" is actually a cluster of many small flowers. The center of a sunflower is made up of dozens or hundreds of tiny florets, each one a complete flower in miniature. Each floret contains only a small drop of nectar, but because so many florets are crowded close together, a hummingbird taps many in a short time, making a visit to a sunflower worth the effort.

Q Why do only female ruby-throated hummingbirds show up at the feeder on my back porch?

Jamie Viebach NEW LENOX, ILLINOIS

Kenn and Kimberly: Male and female ruby-throateds don't ever stay together as pairs. The male has a small territory where he courts any passing female and chases away other males. The female has her own home range, where she raises her young. If a female ruby-throated has her nest nearby, she may come to your feeder regularly; if the neighborhood male's center of activity is farther away, he may be getting his food elsewhere. So in early summer, it's partly a matter of luck.

Q How can I keep my homemade hummingbird sugar water from molding so quickly?

Della Lansdell

PRATTVILLE, ALABAMA

Kenn and Kimberly: We suggest mixing your own using 4 parts water to 1 part sugar, and bringing it to a full boil to break down the sugar completely. Once it's cool, refrigerate what you don't use between fillings. Avoid using red dye; the birds don't need it, and it's easier to monitor the freshness of colorless sugar water. Another way to avoid mold is to fill feeders only halfway and clean them before each refill.

Q What can I plant in baskets to hang near my hummingbird feeder? It's mostly sunny and I don't want them to be too heavy.

Barbara Wiser DODGE CITY, ALABAMA

Melinda: You have quite a few options. Petunias look great in hanging baskets, and many of the new varieties require less deadheading. Another longtime favorite, geranium, will help attract hummingbirds, too; look for heat tolerant varieties like Maverick and Orbit. Or grow Blizzard, Cascade or Summer Series ivy geraniums that can take the heat. Bidens and lantana have lovely flowers, tolerate heat well and look nice in hanging baskets. Cupheas such as firecracker plant and bat face are real hummingbird magnets and usually thrive in your climate.

Q How can I keep larger birds like orioles from monopolizing my hummingbird feeders?

Roger Hatfield DEL RIO, TEXAS

Kenn and Kimberly: In your region of Texas, you're lucky to have several kinds of orioles, but we understand why you'd want to keep space open for hummingbirds. One approach is to have one or two "sacrificial" feeders, with perches that make it easy for orioles and other larger birds to drink sugar water. If you have other feeders with no perches, the hummingbirds can still hover at those to feed, ideally undisturbed by the larger birds.

Baltimore oriole

Q How can I keep yellow jackets away from my hummingbird feeders?

Gail Mitchell MARTINSVILLE, VIRGINIA

Kenn and Kimberly: Reducing the ratio of sugar to water might help. Try 5 parts water to 1 part sugar, instead of the usual 4-to-1 ratio. Be sure to clean any spillage off the feeding ports after refilling the feeder. Another option is to use saucer-style feeders that keep nectar farther away from the feeding ports. Because bees and wasps prefer to feed in sunny areas, you could try moving your feeders to a shadier area. Avoid using products such as pesticides, petroleum jelly or cooking oil on the feeding ports to discourage bees and wasps, since these substances can be deadly for hummingbirds. It's also good to remember that these insects are important pollinators, and we should protect them, too.

Q Hummingbirds visit my feeders every day, year-round. Where do they sleep at night in chilly weather, and how do they survive the cold?

Kay Teseniar KELSO, WASHINGTON

Kenn and Kimberly: Hummingbirds will often find a twig that's sheltered from the wind to rest on for the night. Also, in winter they can enter a deep sleeplike state known as torpor. All body functions slow dramatically; metabolism drops by as much as 95 percent, and heart rate and body temperature decline significantly. Torpor lets hummingbirds conserve precious energy and survive surprisingly low temperatures. In spite of their fragile appearance, they're tough little critters!

Anna's
hummingbird

Q My hummingbird feeders never have visitors. What is the best type to buy or build?

Lothar Willertz SANFORD, MICHIGAN

Kenn and Kimberly: The traditional glass bottle that threads into a plastic basin works extremely well. We prefer the 30-ounce bottle because it's more stable and doesn't tip as easily when orioles drink from it. We also like the type with a shallow plastic basin where the lid with feeding ports snaps down over it. Both are easy to clean, and that is important. Before giving up on the feeders, make sure you use the proper recipe of 4 parts water to 1 part sugar. If the mixture is too weak, birds won't be interested.

Q Is this hummingbird taking a nap? It landed on this branch after feeding, leaned back for about a minute and then took off!

Charles Hoysa WARRENTON, VIRGINIA

Kenn and Kimberly: You probably caught your visitor preening or in midstretch. With super long bills and tiny feet, hummingbirds strike pretty odd poses while preening their feathers. Hummingbirds also stretch, just like we do when we get up from the table after a meal. Sometimes they will pause in an odd pose and hold it for up to a minute, for no obvious reason.

Q A female ruby-throat built a nest and incubated her eggs. She abandoned the nest when a male showed up. Why?

Joseph Salmieri

LINDENWOLD, NEW JERSEY

Kenn and Kimberly: Although it's always guesswork with this kind of situation, we think the timing was probably a coincidence. It's true that a male ruby-throated can be aggressive, but the female is a very tough and tenacious mother dedicated to caring for her nest. In most cases, she wouldn't be driven away by an obnoxious new boy in the neighborhood. It's unfortunate that the female in your yard abandoned her nest, but there was probably some other cause.

Q This hummingbird (below) visited my yard. I believe it is a juvenile ruby-throated or Anna's, but it's so small. Can you help?

Jim Mcclellan SAN DIEGO, CALIFORNIA

Kenn and Kimberly: Nice close-up! It's amazing how small these birds can look when you get close. But this is actually an adult male, not a juvenile. The adult male Anna's hummingbird is the only hummer in North America that has red on the throat and on the top of the head. Anna's is the most common hummingbird along the California coast, and it's found there year-round. Ruby-throated hummingbirds, so common in the East, are extremely rare visitors to California, with only a few ever recorded.

Q I use about a gallon of sugar water every day. Is it possible to determine how many hummingbirds I feed by the amount of sugar water they drink in a day?

Marge Kaufman SIGEL, ILLINOIS

Kenn and Kimberly: According to lab studies, the amount of sugar water consumed by a hummingbird will vary depending on the richness of the sugar concentration. With the typical 4-to-1 ratio of water to sugar, a ruby-throated probably won't drink more than about 2 fluid ounces per day. A gallon of sugar water could feed about 60 hummingbirds in a day! The actual number of individuals could be even higher if some are just stopping briefly, or it could be lower if some of the sugar water is being lost to evaporation, dripping, insects or other factors. It's tricky to come up with solid numbers, but it's still fun to ponder how many hummers might be out there.

Ruby-throated hummingbirds

Female
broad-tailed
hummingbird

Q After watching hummingbirds at my feeders, I noticed that males put their bills farther into the sugar water than females. Do females have longer bills?

Pat Comack HAZELWOOD, MISSOURI

Kenn and Kimberly: That's an interesting observation! Female ruby-throated hummingbirds do have a slightly longer bill, on average, than males. The difference is so minor—less than one-tenth of an inch—that most people would never notice. The females also have slightly larger bills overall.

Q When hummingbirds came to feed, this praying mantis reared up and scared the birds away. Why?

Janice Bogott
GERMANTOWN, TENNESSEE

Kenn and Kimberly: Praying mantises do a lot of exploring, and they sometimes wind up perched on hummingbird feeders. Mantises are predators, mostly feeding on smaller insects, and they may catch bees or other bugs attracted to the feeders. However, large mantises have been known to catch and even kill hummingbirds. The mantis in your photo might not have been big enough to capture a ruby-throated, but to be on the safe side, if we find a mantis lurking near one of our feeders, we take it to another spot.

Ruby-throated hummingbirds

LEFT: STEVE AND DAVE MASLOWSKI; FAR RIGHT: ELIJAH GILDEA

Q I never get more than one hummingbird at a time at my feeders. How can I encourage them to share?

Cheryl Vandermark
WALLKILL, NEW YORK

Kenn and Kimberly: Hummingbirds have an instinct to protect their food sources, because in nature, a patch of flowers will produce only so much nectar in a day. The tiny birds carry this defensiveness over to artificial feeders. The best way to keep one hummingbird from dominating a feeder is to put up several feeders in different spots. If some feeders can be out of sight from the others (around a corner, for example), it will be even harder for one bird to control them all. With multiple feeders available, even the more aggressive hummers may give up and just share with others.

Q In early June, this large hummingbird visited my feeder for about three days. I could hear it coming because of its loud chirps. It was almost too big to drink out of the feeder holes. Can you tell me more about it?

Jeanne Wimberley
PIE TOWN, NEW MEXICO

Birds & Blooms editors: The two largest hummingbirds in North America are the blue-throated and the magnificent, both found in the southwestern part of your state. My guess for this is the magnificent because of the heavily spotted breast.

Q Do you have any tips for keeping hummingbird nectar from freezing? We have several birds that stay all winter.

Laurie Black SALEM, OREGON

Kenn and Kimberly: In your area of Oregon, Anna's hummingbirds appear year-round. They seem to be among the toughest members of the family, surviving very cold weather if they get enough to eat. To keep feeders from freezing, we have experimented with hanging them next to the house and putting a heat lamp above them. It worked well when we had a wintering rufous hummingbird in Ohio. You can also bring feeders inside at night, but it's important to put them back out first thing in the morning, because the hummers need a shot of energy after a cold night.

An Anna's hummingbird braves the winter.

Female ruby-throated hummingbird with coneflower

Q I'd like to create and maintain a hummingbird retreat in my backyard. What perennials should I be planting?

Michael Gorss

CENTERVILLE, MASSACHUSETTS

Melinda: Create a garden area filled with hummingbird favorites in a sheltered location. Include spring, summer and fall bloomers to provide three seasons of nectar for these flying beauties. For early blooming, plant bleeding heart, columbine, coral bells and iris. Good summer bloomers are daylilies, penstemon, garden phlox, perennial hibiscus, bee balm, salvia and cardinal flower. Finish off the season with gayfeather (*Liatris*) and coneflower. Add a few vines like clematis and native honeysuckle vine for vertical interest and more hummingbird appeal. For more plant picks, visit our website: *birdsandblooms.com*.

Q This is one of two hummingbirds (below) that visit every September. Is it an immature male? At what age do hummingbirds get their full coloring?

Lynn Smith LEAGUE CITY, TEXAS

Birds & Blooms editors: Yes, the hummingbirds you're seeing are most likely immature male ruby-throateds. By the time immature hummingbirds return to their nesting grounds in the U.S. in spring, they are in full adult plumage. The ones you noted were probably hatched a couple of months earlier and were migrating through your yard on their way to wintering grounds in the tropics.

Q By feeding the hummingbirds, how much are we helping them? If I didn't feed these little birds, would it matter?

Lynda Franco BUFFALO, MISSOURI

Birds & Blooms editors: If you totally stopped feeding the hummingbirds, they would survive just fine. Studies have shown that wild birds glean only a small percentage of their daily food from feeders. I'm sure there are others in your neighborhood who would pick up the slack should you stop feeding. Don't worry about birds becoming dependent on your feeders. We feed birds for our own pleasure, not for the health and prosperity of the birds.

Female
ruby-throated
hummingbird

Q Hummingbirds refuse to eat the sugar water I make with organic sugar. Can you explain the difference between organic and white?

Christine Davis LUDLOW, MASSACHUSETTS

Kenn and Kimberly: Pure white table sugar is the safest option for mixing homemade nectar for hummingbirds. Many consider organic sugar, which doesn't tend to be fully refined to pure sucrose, unsafe for feeding hummingbirds.

Q On an early summer evening, I was sitting on the patio and saw a female ruby-throated hummingbird at some coral bells. A male appeared and they flew together, spiraling into the air about 75 feet! Is this a mating ritual?

Jenifer Junkins TORONTO, ALABAMA

Kenn and Kimberly: We wish we could say that the male was just being romantic, but it's more likely that he was trying to chase her away. Male ruby-throateds are combative little guys, and when they've found a good patch of flowers, they usually respond to others of their kind by trying to chase them away. If the other hummer is a male, they may have a brief fight before one of them leaves. If the intruder is a female, the male may start by chasing and then gradually shift over to something that looks more like courtship displays.

Q What is this (below)? It moves as though it's a hummingbird but looks like a moth. Several of them visit my butterfly bushes.

Peggy Schafer IONIA, MICHIGAN

Kenn and Kimberly: Yes, this is a type of moth called a hummingbird clearwing. They are in the sphinx moth or hawk moth family, and many of them hover at flowers just like hummingbirds. The majority of sphinx moths are active only at night, but clearwings visit blooms in the daytime. Their yellow and black bodies may suggest the color pattern of a bumblebee, which could help to protect them from predators, and they also move very fast. You did well to get such a good photo!

Q I thought this was a hummingbird, but when it settled on the flower, I realized it wasn't. What is it?

Travis Stelly SUNSET, LOUISIANA

Kenn and Kimberly: This dusky little gem is called a long-tailed skipper. The skippers make up a very distinctive group of butterflies, mostly small with stout bodies and very fast flight. Several of them have an extended "tail" on the hindwing, but the one that's officially known as long-tailed skipper also has some iridescent blue-green at the base of the wings. In your fine photo, some of that color is visible on the abdomen and on the top of the skipper's head. Long-tailed skippers are mostly tropical, but they're also common in the southeastern states.

Q My husband and I can't decide if the bird (below) is a juvenile broad-tailed or black-chinned hummingbird. What do you think?

Debbie Whiting MIDLAND, TEXAS

Kenn and Kimberly: Female and immature hummingbirds are among the most challenging of all birds to identify—even with a great photo like this! We can be sure that this isn't a black-chinned, because it shows too much of an orange tinge on the sides and near the tail. However, we can't be positive that the bird is a broad-tailed, either. Another possibility is that it might be a young female rufous hummingbird. Rufous hummingbirds are regular migrants through your area, and their "fall" migration begins as early as the end of June, although the young birds are more likely to come through in late July and August. So it could be a juvenile or a female. From this photo, there's no way of knowing for sure.

Q What is the best hummingbird feeder and how should I present it (height, location, etc.)?

Barent Parslow STAUNTON, VIRGINIA

Kenn and Kimberly: For the most part, hummingbirds aren't picky, so the best feeder is the one you find easiest to fill, clean and hang. Since they're accustomed to hovering low in front of flowers, there's no real height requirement. Just make sure the feeder is in a place where it's easy to see and enjoy! This will allow you to monitor it closely for filling and cleaning, too.

Q We were finally successful in attracting ruby-throated hummingbirds with feeders. Now that we've attracted them, will the same group and their offspring return to our backyard next year?

Dennis Woods GREENSVILLE, ONTARIO

Kenn and Kimberly: Now that you've had success in attracting the ruby-throateds, there's a good chance they'll come back every year. Young hummingbirds usually return to the general area where they were hatched. In addition, hummingbirds have strong spatial memory, and they may return to the same spots where they've found food in the past, even after migrating thousands of miles. If you have feeders and flowers ready at the right season, you can expect to have plenty of hummingbirds.

MEET THE EXPERTS

Kenn and Kimberly Kaufman are the duo behind the Kaufman Field Guide series. They speak and lead bird trips all over the world.

Melinda Myers is a nationally known, award-winning garden expert, TV/radio host and author of more than 20 books.

CHAPTER 8

DIY Projects

A little creativity goes a long way when it comes to making hummingbirds happy. We show you how to fashion your own feeders, misters and more using household items.

A Bottle for Hummingbirds

With just a few bucks and a recycled glass bottle, you can make a great feeder. You'll be amazed at how fun and easy it is. And with the copper accents, it's a decorative addition to your backyard, too.

Supplies

- Glass bottle
- 5 ft. of 4-gauge untreated copper wire
- 3 to 5 ft. of 12-gauge untreated copper wire
- Hummingbird feeding tube
- Beads or other decorations
- D-ring or carabiner
- Screw eye
- File
- Needle-nose pliers
- Wire cutter

Instructions

Step 1. File the ends of the copper wires so there are no sharp edges.

St ep 2. Take the 4-gauge wire and bend it at 1 end to form a small circle. This circle should fit loosely over the opening of the bottle.

Step 3. Insert the bottle in the circle, and make 1 more loop around the neck to hold securely.

Step 4. With the neck of the bottle securely in the 2 loops, wind the rest of the wire around the bottle. (You have a little freedom to create your own design.) The wire should be loose enough to easily remove the bottle for refilling the sugar water, but tight enough to hold the feeder securely.

Step 5. Bend the last 18 inches or so of wire upward to make a hanging hook and then fashion a loop at the very end to secure it, as shown.

Step 6. Next, decorate your feeder using the 12-gauge copper wire.

Step 7. Use needle-nose pliers and wire cutters to shape the wire as needed. Here's a design tip: To create the look of curling vines, wrap the wire around a pencil first and then attach it in pieces.

Step 8. Use colorful beads or other adornments to complete your design. Remember, hummingbirds love red, so it's a fine accent color.

Step 9. Remove the bottle and fill with sugar water. Gently twist the stopper of the store-bought feeding tube into place at the opening of the bottle. It should fit snugly to avoid leaking.

Step 10. After you fill it with sugar water, place the bottle back into the copper holder. You might have to shake the bottle a little to dislodge any air bubbles. If it leaks, remove the feeding tube and try repositioning the stopper to get a snugger fit.

Step 11. Ready to put your feeder to work? Make sure it hangs securely by hooking the feeder onto a snap ring or carabiner. Put the ring through a screw eye and hang the entire feeder in the desired location. Then sit back, relax and watch for hummingbirds. Change the sugar water every few days.

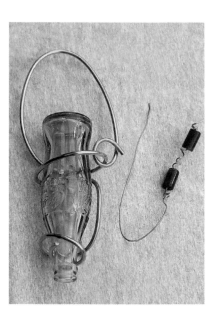

CHOOSING A BOTTLE

Glass bottles larger than 375 ml are heavy and more prone to leakage. Thus, they are not recommended for this project. Above all, the bottle must provide a tight fit for the stopper portion of the feeding tube you buy. Anything less than an airtight fit will allow the nectar to drip from the feeding tube. Many soda and water bottles are a good fit for a commercial tube feeder assembly. Be sure to test the seal before you complete your design and add sugar water.

PVC Pipe Feeder

Create this whimsical hummingbird feeder with materials you can find at your local hardware and craft stores. Decorate it in your favorite colors and the piece will serve double duty as a bird feeder and work of art.

Supplies

- Three 9-in. lengths of ¾-in. PVC piping, each with threading at one end only
- 6 PVC caps (3 slip, 3 threaded)
- Plumber's seal tape (if necessary)
- PVC adhesive
- Fine steel wool
- Drill and small bit
- Spray paint
- ½-in. masking or painter's tape
- 14-gauge copper wire
- Glass beads
- Fabric or plastic (optional)

Instructions

Step 1. Using steel wool, lightly sand the pipe pieces and caps, including the insides of the slip caps.

Step 2. Attach slip caps to the non-threaded end of the pipes with PVC adhesive. Allow to dry.

Step 3. Drill a small hole in each piece of piping about 3 in. from the capped end.

Step 4. Paint the PVC pipe. Prime it first or use a spray paint with primer. Spray on a base color and allow to dry. Create stripes by taping off a candy cane pattern or other design and spraying with a second color. Create a zigzag stripe (as shown) by applying tape in the opposite direction of the first stripe and spraying with a third color. Allow each paint layer to dry completely before removing the tape.

Step 5. Once paint is dry, wash pipes with mild soap and warm water to remove any paint odor or residue.

Step 6. Cut a 22-in. length of wire and fold it in half, leaving an eye hook at the top. Twist the wire 5 times, add a glass bead and twist 5 more times. Wrap the 2 strands of wire around center of 1 pipe, twist 5 times, add a glass bead and twist 5 more times. Repeat for remaining pipes.

Step 7. To finish, hang the pipe pieces together, trim 1 wire at the end of the last twist, leaving a 1-in. tail on the other wire. Bend the tail into a C-shape to link the feeders together; flatten the C slightly with a hammer so the copper will hold its shape. To hang pieces individually, make a decorative swirl with both wire ends (as shown at center and far right) and flatten it all out with a hammer.

Step 8. Line everything up and tighten the wire around the tube. Tighten the twists until the tube is level and the hole faces up.

Step 9. If desired, make a flower out of fabric or plastic in your color of choice. Put a hole in the center and glue to the outside of the feeding port.

Step 10. Test the feeder with water: Fill at the threaded end and close with a threaded cap. If it leaks, wrap the pipe threads with seal tape.

Step 11. Fill the feeder with nectar or sugar water, placing your finger over the feeding hole to prevent spilling. Seal with the threaded cap and hang with the feeding hole facing up.

Once your feeder is in place, rotate the pipe up so the sugar water doesn't spill out!

Hummingbird Mister

This easy-to-make water feature is irresistible to hummers. Why? As some of the zippiest birds around, they don't stop all that often to sit in a birdbath—but they love water. So give them some refreshing mist instead. It all adds charm to your yard.

Supplies

- 5-gallon plastic container, about 20 x 16 x 12 in.
- 2 unthreaded ½-in. PVC pipes, 14 in. and 15 in. long
- 1 threaded ½-in. PVC pipe, 18 in. long
- 2 PVC elbows for ½-in. pipe
- 1 PVC cap for ½-in. pipe
- PVC cement
- Steel wool
- Submersible pump
- Small rocks
- One ½-in.-female-to-⅝-in.-male adapter
- 3 misters

Instructions

Step 1. Start by cutting the unthreaded PVC pipe. (You can use pipe cutters or a handsaw.) You'll need a 14-in. piece for the left leg and a 15-in. piece for the top.

Step 2. In the 15-in. piece, drill 1 hole in the center for the top mister and 2 holes for the bottom misters. The size of the sprayers will determine the size of the holes you drill. See the photo at right for a close look at how the misters fit in.

Step 3. The third piece of PVC, for the right leg, should be threaded at both ends. This piece is likely precut to 18 in. long. You'll want to cut this to roughly 12 in., but first do a little measuring. Attach the adapter to the end of the threaded pipe and pump. Meanwhile, place the cap on the left leg. Stand both legs up so they're even. Mark the top of the right leg to mimic the length of the left leg and make your cut. (Once everything is attached, you'll have a large U.)

Step 4. It's time to attach all the plumbing pieces together. First rub the ends of the PVC pipe and the insides of the PVC elbows and cap with steel wool. This will help the pieces adhere together. Dust the pieces off, apply PVC adhesive to the outside of the pipe, and connect the elbows and cap. Be sure the holes you drilled face up and down. Let adhesive dry.

Step 5. Remove sprayers and adapter from the piping, and lightly sand the pipes with steel wool. Start with a coat of primer on the piping and let dry. Prime your container, too, if needed.

Step 6. Once the primer is dry, paint the piping and container with the color of your choice.

Step 7. After all the paint is dry, it's time to get creative. Paint flowers or your choice of design with acrylic paint. When complete, spray your work with a clear matte finishing spray.

Step 8. Now it's time to insert the misters. Use a toothpick to add a pea-size amount of cement to the base of the misters. Insert into the drilled holes, making sure not to clog any sprayer openings. Allow cement to dry.

Step 9. Use the adapter to connect the piping to the pump. (If the seal isn't tight, you might need to add thread seal tape.) Place the adapter inside the container and secure it in place with bricks or small rocks that you find around your yard.

Step 10. Set the mister outside near a feeder or flowers, and add water. While your flying friends might not splash around for long, they'll enjoy a moment of refreshment!

The pump we used is an EcoPlus Eco-100 Submersible Pump. If you're looking for something similar, make sure you use a pump that transfers roughly 100 gallons of water per hour. This will ensure a good mist.

Metal Yard Art

Use your imagination to create a bird sculpture out of an old light fixture.

Supplies

- Assorted disassembled lamp pieces
- 2 tin cans
- Snips
- Needle-nose pliers
- Hole punch
- Hammer
- Flower stake

Instructions

Step 1. Play with the disassembled lamp pieces by arranging them in different ways to see what your final bird might look like. Choose a favorite combination.

Step 2. A lamp rod is what holds everything together. Drill a hole in a finial (the fancy topper) if it doesn't already have one, and slide it and a few more pieces onto the rod to create the bird's head. (Don't forget to leave some extra lamp rod for the rest of the body.) Then, secure a flower stake to the rod.

Step 3. Now it's time to make the wings. Cut 1 long, wing-shaped piece from a tin can, punch a hole in the center and slide it onto the rod. We bent the metal wings on our hummingbird to make it look as if it's flying. Secure the wings in place and slide on a couple of pieces to round out the body.

Step 4. Cut 2 tail feathers from a tin can and slide them onto the lamp rod. Use a washer with a nut to tighten the feathers against the body.

Step 5. Prevent rust by spraying it with clear lacquer or acrylic sealer. Stake it in the garden or a planter.

INSPIRING IDEAS

Animal sculptures can be made from all sorts of household items.

Broken Yard Tools
Shovels, stiff or flexible rakes, wooden handles and smaller hand tools are great for tails, heads, bodies, wings and feet for larger yard sculptures.

Plumbing Parts
Supply hoses, valves, bathtub and sink handles, hose bibs, threaded pipes and a vast array of brass fittings are easy to assemble into an animal.

Furnace and Gas Fittings
Copper furnace supply lines or black metal gas pipes and fittings can be ideal animal armatures.

Electrical Supplies
Metal conduit and fittings, copper wire, fuses, plugs, lamp parts, worn-out circuit breakers and even outlet covers can be repurposed.

Hardware and Tin Cans
Magnets, nuts and bolts, and other hardware attached to tin cans create whimsical creatures. Door hinges, big bolts, springs, doorknobs and a host of other everyday hardware are sources for animal inspiration.

Hummingbird Swing

Talk about a perch with personality. Give your friendly fliers somewhere to rest with a handmade swing made with simple materials.

Supplies

- Twigs, various sizes
- 20- and 18-gauge wire
- Beads
- Wire cutters
- Round-nosed pliers
- Pencil or toothpick
- Flat-nosed pliers

Instructions

Step 1. Soak twigs in water until they become pliable.

Step 2. Using a 6- to 7-in. twig for swing base, lash 1 end of a longer twig to 1 side of base with a 12-in. piece of 20-gauge wire, using round-nosed pliers to twist wire. Gently bend twig and lash other end to opposite side of base.

Step 3. Twist any remaining wire into tendrils by winding tail around a pencil or toothpick. Remove pencil and pull at end of wire with flat-nosed pliers to achieve desired look.

Step 4. Cut a 12- to 18-in. piece of 20-gauge wire. Wrap 1 end around arch of twig to secure. Add colored beads (red beads are a hummingbird favorite). Twist beaded wire around twig and secure end. Repeat process at intervals along twig arch as desired.

Step 5. Cut an 18-in. piece of 18-gauge wire. Wrap 1 end around the top of arch, working piece into a decorative loop to use as a hanger and adding any beads as desired. Wrap other end around top of arch.

Step 6. Hang outdoors.

Grow for Your Zone

Find the number associated with your region, and
then stick to plants that will thrive in your area.

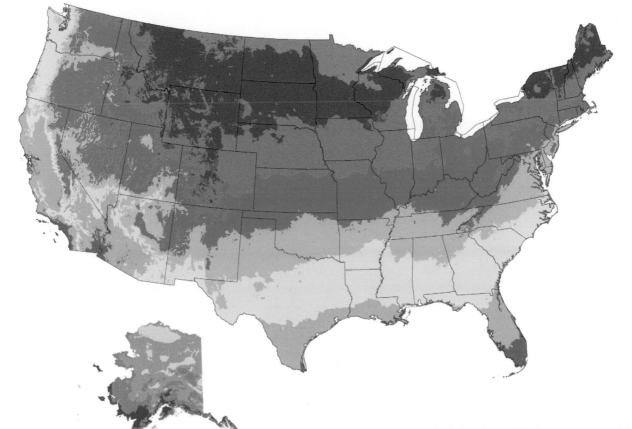

ALASKA

HAWAII

USDA PLANT HARDINESS ZONES

Hardiness zones reflect the average annual
minimum cold temperatures for an area. If it's
difficult to precisely locate your city on the map
here, use the interactive version on the USDA's
website, *planthardiness.ars.usda.gov*. Enter your
ZIP code, and your hardiness zone and average
minimum winter temperature range will appear.

AVERAGE ANNUAL EXTREME MINIMUM TEMPERATURE

Temp (F)	Zone	Temp (C)
-60 to -50	1	-51.1 to -45.6
-50 to -40	2	-45.6 to -40
-40 to -30	3	-40 to -34.4
-30 to -20	4	-34.4 to -28.9
-20 to -10	5	-28.9 to -23.3
-10 to 0	6	-23.3 to -17.8
0 to 10	7	-17.8 to -12.2
10 to 20	8	-12.2 to -6.7
20 to 30	9	-6.7 to -1.1
30 to 40	10	-1.1 to 4.4
40 to 50	11	4.4 to 10
50 to 60	12	10 to 15.6
60 to 70		15.6 to 21.1

Move, Mantis!

I thought it strange that this hummingbird kept circling this flower but never landed. Then I noticed the praying mantis hiding beneath the bloom. I quickly (and safely) moved the mantis to another location so the hummingbird could land on the flower without fear.

Michele Carter NEWPORT, NORTH CAROLINA

Birds&Blooms